국제학회 English 구두발표

연구발표를 위한 영어 프레젠테이션

C.S. Langham 저
정 원 균 · 최 나 래 역

PRESENTATION UPDATE:

A GUIDE TO STARTING, CHANGING FORMAL ENGLISH TO INFORMAL ENGLISH, IMPROVING SLIDES, ENHANCING THE CLARITY OF THE MAIN BODY, FINISHING, CREATING A CLEAR SUMMARY SLIDE, AND WRITING AN AUDIENCE-FRIENDLY SCRIPT

대한나래출판사

DaehanNarae Publishing, Inc.

SK V1 Tower 1507
Younmujang 5 gagil 25, Sungdong-gu,
Seoul 04782, Korea
TEL: +82-2-922-7080
FAX: +82-2-922-0841
E-mail: nrpub@naver.com
Website: www.nrbooks.kr

国際学会 English 口頭発表 研究発表のための英語プレゼンテーション
C.S. Langham 著
医歯薬出版株式会社 (東京), 2019.

This book was originally published in Japanese under the title of:
Presentation Update
by: C.S. Langham
© 2019 1st edition
ISHIYAKU PUBLISHERS, INC.
7-10, Honkomagome 1 chome, Bunkyo-ku,
Tokyo 113-8612, Japan

국제학회 English 구두발표 – 연구발표를 위한 영어 프레젠테이션

발행일 2023년 7월 5일
저자 C.S. Langham
역자 정원균, 최나래
발행인 최용원
편집디자인 김애선
표지디자인 김애선
교정·교열 염정혜
발행처 **대한나래출판사** (등록 제2012-000051호/1994.6.10)
주소 서울시 성동구 연무장 5가길 25, 성수역 SK V1 Tower 1507호
전화 (02) 922-7080
팩스 (02) 922-0841
이메일 nrpub@naver.com
홈페이지 www.nrbooks.kr

ISBN 978-89-5741-956-4

정가 30,000원

Printed in Korea

Introduction

This book is for people who need to give oral presentations in English. It is written in English and has section titles and short summaries of the main points in Japanese. The contents can be used in most fields and situations. My intention has been to provide a highly practical guide with numerous examples. I have attempted to make the material as accessible as possible and have avoided long explanations.

This book covers the following topics: **starting a presentation, using informal English that is suitable for an oral presentation, simple ways of improving slides, improving clarity in the main body of the presentation, finishing your presentation,** and **creating clear summary slides and an audience-friendly script.**

I would stress that readers should not feel they have to use all of the advice and examples in this book. It is necessary to be selective and choose the material that fits your presentation. I hope that readers of this book will find the contents useful and be able to improve their presentations.

Clive Langham

C.S. Langham

ABOUT THE AUTHOR

Clive Langham is from the United Kingdom. He is a professor at Nihon University School of Dentistry. He has taught English in the UK, Indonesia, Saudi Arabia and, since 1985, in Japan. His research interests include scientific English, and the language of presentations.

- 1976년 Huddersfield 대학교 졸업
- 1982년 Kent 대학교 대학원 수료
- 2000년 일본대학 치학부 교수 (영어)
- 2020년 일본대학 특임교수

Acknowledgments

Thanks are due to my colleagues at the Journal of Oral Science, particularly Professor N. Koshikawa, Editor in Chief, who has shown an interest in my work. I am indebted to Dr. Noriko Yamaguchi of the Institute of Agro-environmental Sciences for allowing access to presentation material. I also wish to acknowledge my colleague and friend, Brian Purdue of Tsukuba University, who has been a constant source of inspiration. Additionally, I have received support and advice from Michio Tajima and Minoru Hirata at Nihon University School of Dentistry. Finally, I wish to acknowledge the participants on presentation skills programs at the National Institute of Advanced Industrial Science and Technology and Tsukuba Center for Institutes.

Clive Langham
Nihon University
School of Dentistry
Ochanomizu, Tokyo
December 1st, 2019

역 자 의 글

이 책은 2019년 말에 일본에서 발간된 원저(国際学会 English 口頭発表, 研究発表のための英語プレゼンテーション)를 우리말로 옮긴 역서입니다. 저자이신 클라이브 랭햄(C.S. Langham) 교수께서는 영국에서 공부하신 분으로, 현재는 도쿄에 소재한 일본대학교 치과대학에 재직하며 영어 교육을 담당하고 있다고 합니다.

이 원저는 책의 제목처럼, 연구자가 국제학회에서 영어로 구두발표를 할 때 매우 요긴하게 활용할 수 있는 구어체 표현을 폭넓게 다루고 있습니다. 책상머리에서 논문을 작성할 때 사용하는 문어체의 영어는 그 틀이 비교적 정형화되어 있지만, 외국인 청중들이 지켜보는 국제학회에서 구어체의 영어로 자연스럽게 의사소통을 하는 일은 엄청난 고역이 아닐 수 없습니다. 따라서 국제학회의 영어 구두발표를 앞두고 온갖 근심에 싸여 있을 연구자에게는 이 책이 밝은 햇살 같은 길잡이가 될 것입니다. 또한 이 책의 내용이 특정한 학문 또는 연구 분야에 한정되지 않기 때문에 자연과학이나 보건의료 등의 거의 모든 연구 분야에서 응용될 수 있기도 합니다.

우리나라의 학술 수준과 연구 역량이 세계적으로 비약함으로써 국제학회에서 그 성과를 공유하는 일이 이제는 특별하지도 않게 되었습니다. 하지만 우리에게는 영어라는 언어적 장벽이 여전히 큰 숙제이기도 합니다. 아무쪼록 이 역서가 국제학회의 구두발표를 준비하느라 머리를 싸매고 노심초사하고 있을 발표자에게 도움이 되길 바랍니다.

정 원 균

정 원 균

- 연세대학교 치과대학, 동 대학원 졸업(치의학박사)
- 치과보존과 전문의
- 전, 21세기치과병원 원장
- 현, 연세대학교 치위생학과 교수

최 나 래

- 연세대학교 치위생학과, 동 보건대학원 졸업(병원경영학석사)
- 현, 서울대학교 치과병원 보건직 치과위생사

Contents

Part 4 How to improve the clarity of the main body 101

본론을 알기 쉽게 전달하는 방법

논리적으로 내용을 전개하는 표현, 슬라이드의 정보를 설명하는 표현, 본론(main body) 설명하는 데 필요한 표현과 예문을 소개한다.

Columns

Part 1

Starting

발표를 시작하는 방법

Starting is one of the most important parts of your presentation. You have about a minute to introduce yourself, give the title of your presentation, and explain the material you will cover. In this section, I show how to start.

구두발표를 시작할 때는 먼저 좌장에게 감사 인사를 하고, 자신의 소속과 이름을 밝힌 후에 발표의 주제와 개요를 간략히 소개한다. 이때 발표의 전체 구성을 한 장으로 정리한 '목차 슬라이드'를 제시할 수도 있다. 이 장에서는 발표를 시작할 때 자주 사용하는 표현과 예문을 소개한다.

1 Thank the Chairperson
좌장에게 감사 인사

Here are some examples of how to thank the Chairperson.

소개해주셔서 감사합니다.

1. Thank you.
2. Thank you, Chair.
3. Thank you, Chairperson.
4. Thank you, Professor Williams.
5. Thank you for the introduction.
6. Thank you for your kind introduction.

가장 간단한 1의 표현을 사용하는 것이 좋다. 학회의 구두발표에서는 가능한 한 짧게 말하는 것이 바람직하다.

Example 1 is better because it is shorter and easier to say.

Common errors – 흔히 하는 실수

At a domestic conference I attended, several presenters started like this.

✕ Thank you ***for the*** Chairperson.

*Thank you for the chairperson*이라고 말하면 잘못된 표현이다. **Thank you for** 뒤에는 **the introduction** 또는 **your question** 등과 같이 사람이 아니라 어떤 행위를 붙여서 말해야 한다.

This sentence is incorrect. The expression, **thank you for**, is used like this.

○ Thank you **for the introduction**.
○ Thank you **for your kind introduction**.

In the question and answer session, **Thank you for**, is used like this.

○ **Thank you for** your question.
○ **Thank you for** the question.

2 State your name and affiliation
발표자의 이름과 소속 밝히기

Many presenters use difficult expressions and make basic grammatical mistakes when **stating their name and affiliation.** Here is a quick, easy to use example.

발표자가 자신의 이름과 소속을 밝힐 때 너무 어려운 표현이나 잘못된 문법으로 말하는 경우가 많다.

저는 ○○대학교 △△학과의 ~라고 합니다.

- Thank you. **My name is** Ken Watanabe. **I'm with** London University. **I'm in** the Department of Informatics.

The presenter introduces his/her affiliation using the simple expression, **I'm with** + affiliation.
It is also possible to say,

- **I work at** Osaka General Hospital.
- **I'm working at** Osaka General Hospital.
- **I'm at** Osaka General Hospital.

자신이 소속된 대학, 연구기관, 병원 등을 말할 때는 **I'm with ~** 또는 **I work at ~**이라는 표현을 사용한다.

Please note that the word **department** is introduced with the preposition **in.**

- **I'm in** the Department of Informatics.
- **I'm in** the Department of Community Health.

학부 또는 학과의 소속은 **I'm in**으로 표현한다.

You can combine the following two sentences like this.

(1) I'm with London University. (2) I'm in the Department of Informatics.

(1+2) **I'm with** London University **in the** Department of Informatics.

I'm with (+ 대학 이름)과 in (+ 학부 이름 또는 학과 이름)을 한 문장으로 표현할 수도 있다.

Using the words **with** and **in**, you can state your affiliation quickly and easily in a single sentence.

Common errors – 흔히 하는 실수

✕ I am *staff* at Newcastle University.
✕ I am *a staff* at Newcastle University.
○ **I am a member of staff** at Newcastle University.

✕ I *work* Newcastle University.
○ **I work at** Newcastle University.

✕ I *work for* Newcastle University.
○ **I'm with** Newcastle University.

The verb **work for** is usually used with a company name, not a university or institute. Here is an example. **I work for Toyota**.

✕ I *belong to* Newcastle University.
○ **I'm with** Newcastle University.

✕ I'm *from* Newcastle University.
○ **I'm with** Newcastle University.

The pattern **I'm from** should not be used when stating your affiliation.
Please note that the following sentences using the word **from** are correct and can be used in general conversation.

○ **A speaker from London University** gave a very impressive presentation.
○ **There are a lot of people from Tokyo University** at this conference.

소속을 말할 때 *I am (a) staff at*이라고 하면 잘못된 표현이다. Staff라는 용어를 사용할 경우라면 I am a member of staff at ~이라고 해야 한다.

Work for ~는 일반적으로 기업의 이름을 말할 때 사용하고, 대학이나 연구기관의 이름에는 사용하지 않는다. 대학의 이름을 말하고 싶을 때는 work at ~으로 해야 한다.

자신이 소속된 대학을 소개할 때 *I'm from (+ 대학 이름)*이라고 하면 안 된다. 다만, 다른 연구자를 언급할 때에는 a speaker from (+ 대학 이름)이라고 표현할 수 있다.

Key points

1. After the Chairperson has introduced you, Thank you is the easiest way of starting.
2. *Thank you for the Chairperson* is incorrect.
3. Save time by stating your affiliation with the short, easy to say expression I'm with + affiliation.
4. If you want to include your department, division, or section, you can use the following sentence.
   - **I'm in + department, division, section.**
5. You can combine the two patterns I'm with + affiliation and I'm in the department of like this.
   - **I'm with London University in the Department of Informatics.**

• 가장 먼저, 좌장에게 감사 인사를 한다. Thank you와 같은 간결한 표현이 바람직하다.

• 이어서 자신의 이름과 소속을 I'm with (+ 대학 이름, 기관 이름), I'm in (+ 학부 이름 또는 학과 이름) 등의 표현으로 소개한다.

3 Handling the title of your presentation
발표 제목의 소개

At domestic conferences in Japan, presenters read their presentation title in full. This wastes time because the title is in the conference handbook, has been announced by the Chairperson, and is also on the first slide. At international conferences, most presenters introduce the topic of their presentation by focusing on 2 or 3 keywords from the title, and do not read the title in full. Here is an example.

공식적인 발표 제목은 프로그램이나 첫 슬라이드에 이미 나와 있으므로 이를 그대로 읽지 않는 편이 좋다. 발표 제목에서 핵심용어(키워드)를 몇 개만 뽑아서 **I'm going to talk about** (+ 핵심용어)라는 방식으로 간결하게 표현하면 된다.

Title

A clinicopathological study of salivary gland cancers

Script

Today, **I'm going to talk about** salivary gland cancers.

왼쪽 예시처럼, 슬라이드의 공식적인 발표 제목보다 짧게 줄여서 말하는 것이 좋다.

The presenter focuses on 3 words from the title, **salivary gland cancers** and introduces the topic with **Today, I'm going to + talk about + topic.**

Here are some more examples of how to introduce the title of your presentation.

오늘은 ~에 관해 말씀드리겠습니다.

- **Today, I'm going to talk about** + 2 or 3 words from the title or a short, simplified version of the title.
- **Today, I will focus on** + 2 or 3 words from the title.
- **My presentation today is on** + 2 or 3 words from the title.
- **My presentation today is about** + 2 or 3 words from the title.
- **This presentation is about** + 2 or 3 words from the title.

3.1 Sentence structures for introducing titles
발표 제목을 소개하는 표현

The following examples show common sentence structures for introducing the topic of your presentation.

- I'm going to talk about (topic)
- I want to talk about (topic)
- I would(I'd) like to talk about (topic)
- I will(I'll) talk about (topic)
- I will(I'll) be talking about (topic)
- My presentation (today) is on (topic)
- This presentation is on (topic)
- My presentation (today) is about (topic)

발표 제목을 소개할 때에는 일반적으로, I'm going to talk about (+ 핵심용어) 등의 표현을 사용한다.

The most frequently used structure is I'm going to talk about + topic.

Note In the above sentences, it is possible to say I'm going to or I am going to. Most native speakers will choose I'm, but it is also correct to say I am. If you are worried about pronunciation and want to avoid I'm or I'd, it is possible to introduce the presentation topic with these sentences.

- My/this presentation is on + topic.
- My/this presentation is about + topic.
- Today, I want to talk about + topic.

I'm, I'd의 단축형 발음에 자신이 없다면 이를 풀어서 I am ~ 또는 I would ~로 말하거나, 왼쪽에 예시된 표현을 사용한다.

3.2 Commonly used verbs for introducing a topic
발표 주제를 소개할 때 사용하는 동사

The three most common verbs for introducing a topic are: talk about, focus on, look at.

talk about ~ 외에도 focus on ~, look at ~ 등을 사용해도 된다.

- **I'm going to talk about** recent developments in orthodontic techniques.
- **I'm going to focus on** the use of CAD/CAM in implant technology.
- **I'm going to look at** the use of CAD/CAM in implant technology.

The most frequent verb for introducing a topic is **talk about**. **Focus on** is also widely used. The verb **look at** is widely used by native speakers. **Look at** is an informal verb.

3.3 How to thank the Chairperson, state your name, affiliation, and topic

좌장에게 인사 → 이름 · 소속의 소개 → 발표 주제의 소개

Here are two examples that include the following 3 functions.

지금까지 설명한 '좌장에 대한 감사 인사, '자신의 이름과 소속의 소개, '발표 주제(제목)의 소개'를 연결하면 아래와 같이 된다.

1. Thanking the chairperson
2. Giving your name, affiliation and department
3. Stating the topic of the presentation

Script(좌장에게 인사 → 이름 · 소속 → 발표 주제의 소개를 위해 작성한 원고의 예)

Example 1

Thank you for the introduction. I'm Neil Smith. I'm with Rutgers University in the Department of Orofacial Pain. Today, I'm going to focus on the trigeminal nerve.

Example 2

Thank you. My name's Chris Jones. I work at the University of Health Sciences in Brisbane. Today, I'll be talking about issues affecting public health.

Common errors — 흔히 하는 실수

✕ ***Today's my topics*** is about development of biodegradable polymers.

There are two errors in this sentence. First, ***today's*** does not need an apostrophe, and **s** should be deleted. Second, ***topics*** does not need an **s** as you will only be talking about one main theme or topic. It is better to change ***topic*** to **presentation** or **talk**. This sentence can be rewritten as follows.

○ **Today, my presentation is on/about** development of biodegradable polymers.

○ **My presentation today is on/about** development of biodegradable polymers.

○ **Today, my talk is on/about** development of biodegradable polymers.

○ **Today, I'm going to talk about / focus on** development of biodegradable polymers.

발표의 주제나 제목을 소개할 때 *Today's my topics is* ~라고 하면 잘못된 표현이다. **Today**에는 소유격 부호를 붙이지 않으며, 발표의 주된 주제 하나에 대해서만 언급할 때는 topic을 단수형으로 사용해야 한다. 이 경우에는 **topic**보다는 **presentation** 또는 **talk**라는 용어를 쓰는 것이 좋다.

Key points

1. At international conferences, presenters do not read the presentation title in full.
2. Introduce your topic by focusing on 2 or 3 keywords that are in the title.
3. The most common sentence for introducing the presentation topic is:
   - **Today, I'm going to talk about + topic.**
4. The most common pattern is: I'm going to
5. The most common verb is talk about. Other frequently used verbs are focus on and look at.

제목 전체를 그대로 읽을 필요는 없다. 제목에서 핵심용어 2~3개를 뽑아 I'm going to talk about (+ 핵심용어) 식의 표현으로 소개한다.

4 Using an overview slide to introduce the structure and contents of your presentation
목차 슬라이드를 활용한 발표 구성의 제시

The purpose of an overview slide is to show the structure and contents of your presentation. Some presenters return to this slide several times during the presentation. Common titles for the overview slide are as follows: **contents, overview, outline**. Please note that the word **contents** is plural and that ***content*** without **s** is incorrect as the title of an overview slide. Also, **overview**, **outline** and **background** should always be singular. You cannot say ***overviews***, ***outlines*** or ***backgrounds***. Overview and outline are always one word.

목차 슬라이드를 활용하여 발표의 전체 구성을 보여 준다. 목차 슬라이드를 발표 시작 때뿐 아니라 발표 도중에도 적절히 활용함으로써 발표의 진행 과정을 점검할 수도 있다.

목차 슬라이드의 제목은 overview, contents, outline 등으로 표현한다. 다만, contents는 반드시 복수형으로 쓰고, overview, outline, background 등은 반드시 단수형으로 사용해야 한다.

4.1 How to introduce an overview slide
목차 슬라이드를 소개하는 방법

Example 1: Here is an overview slide. The script is shown below.

Slide(목차 슬라이드의 예)

Community health interventions for pre-diabetics

Overview

1. Introduction to community health interventions
   - How they work
   - Typical users
2. Interventions for pre-diabetics
   - Face-to-face
   - Online
3. Data from a recent community health project
4. Summary and future directions

This is the supporting script to introduce the overview slide.

Script(앞쪽의 목차 슬라이드를 소개하는 원고의 예)

1. State your name, affiliation, and title of the presentation 이름, 소속, 제목

① Thank you. I'm Ken Wilson. I'm with King's College London in the Department of Community Health. ② I'm going to talk about community health interventions, particularly for people who are pre-diabetic.

2. Introduce the overview slide 목차 슬라이드 소개

③ This is an outline. ④ I'll start with an introduction to community health interventions, focusing on how they work and typical users. ⑤ I'll move on to interventions for pre-diabetics. These are face-to face and also online. ⑥ Then I'll show you some data from a recent community health project. ⑦ I'll finish with a summary and mention future directions.

Note If you want to **add another topic to the overview slide**, use this sentence. **I'll also look at / focus on + topic.** This is the simplest way of adding a topic. You can repeat the same sentence several times.

Key sentences

1. Thank the Chairperson. State your name and affiliation 좌장에게 감사 인사, 이름 · 소속 소개

소개해주셔서 감사합니다. 저는 ~대학의 ~라고 합니다.

- Thank you. I'm Ken Wilson. **I'm with** King's College, London in the Department of Community Health.

Examples

- Thank you. I'm Ken Wilson. **I work at** Kings College, London in the Department of Community Health.
- Thank you. I'm Ken Wilson. **I'm at** Kings College, London in the Department of Community Health.

목차 슬라이드를 소개하기 전에 좌장에게 감사 인사를 하고, 청중에게 자기소개를 한다(2~5쪽 참고).

2. State the topic 발표 주제의 소개

오늘은 ~에 대해 발표하겠습니다.

- I'm going to talk about community health interventions, particularly for people who are pre-diabetic.

Examples

- I'm going to focus on community health interventions.
- I'm going to look at community health interventions.

발표의 주제나 제목의 소개는 6~9쪽을 참고한다.

3. Introduce the overview slide 목차 슬라이드 제시

(목차 슬라이드를 제시하고) 이것이 제가 오늘 말씀드릴 내용입니다.

- This is an outline.

Examples

- This is an overview.
- Here are the contents.
- These are the contents.
- This slide shows the contents.
- These are the points, topics, contents that I am going to cover today.
- Today, I'll be covering these points/topics.
- Today, I'll be covering the following points/topics/contents.
- Today, I'm going to cover these topics.
- These are the topics I'm going to be covering.

목차 슬라이드를 소개할 때 왼쪽과 같은 표현으로 시작한다.

Cover is a useful verb to introduce information in an overview slide. For example, This is an overview. These are the points I am going to cover today. The word cover means talk about, focus on, look at.

목차 슬라이드를 가리키면서 "오늘 이 내용에 대해 말씀드리겠습니다."라고 표현할 때는 동사 cover를 사용하는 것이 좋다.

Note After using any of the sentences in section **3. Introduce the overview slide**, you can then read the information in the overview directly from the powerpoint slide. Please remember to use the pointer as you introduce the points on the slide. Using just one example sentence from section 3. will improve the start of your presentation. It will also help you to start your presentation with confidence.

목차 슬라이드를 제시한 후, 레이저 포인터로 항목을 하나하나 가리키며 읽어가면 된다.

4. Introduce part I of the overview slide

목차 슬라이드 소개 (1)

먼저, ~에 대해서 소개하겠습니다.

- **I'll start with** an introduction to community health interventions, **focusing on** how they work and typical users.

Examples

- **I'll begin with** an introduction to community health interventions, **looking at** how they work and typical users.
- **I'll start by looking at** community health interventions, **focusing on** how they work and typical users.
- **First, I'll introduce** community health interventions, **looking at** how they work and typical users.
- **First, I'll look at** community health interventions, **focusing on** how they work and typical users.
- **First, I'll look at** community health interventions, **concentrating on** how they work and typical users.

'첫 번째 소개할 내용은 ~입니다.'라고 말하고 싶을 때는 **I'll start with an introduction to ~** 등의 표현을 이용한다. **Introduction** 다음에 오는 전치사는 **of**가 아니라 **to**이니 주의해야 한다.

Note I'll begin with an **introduction to** NOT an ***introduction of***. The correct preposition to use with **introduction** is **to**. Here is an example.

- I'll start with **an introduction to** community health interventions.

5. Introduce part 2 of the overview slide
목차 슬라이드 소개 (2)

이어서, ~에 대해 말씀드리겠습니다.

- **I'll move on to** interventions for pre-diabetics. These are face-to-face and also online.

Examples

- **I'll go on to** interventions for pre-diabetics.
- **Next, I'll look at / focus on / describe / explain** interventions for pre-diabetics.

다음 소개로 넘어갈 때는 move on to ~, go on to ~ 등의 표현을 사용하면 좋다.

The useful 3-word verbs **move on to** and **go on to** can be used to introduce the next section / theme / topic / point. The informal 2-word verbs **look at** and **focus on** are also useful for introducing a new topic. Even if you have used **look at** and **focus on** to introduce the title of the presentation, the same verbs can be used here again. Repetition of verbs, such as **look at** and **focus on**, is not an issue.

이 경우에 look at ~, focus on ~ 등의 표현도 활용할 수 있다. 구두발표에서는 이런 동사를 반복해서 사용해도 별문제가 없다(예: 앞에서 look at ~이란 표현을 썼더라도 다음에 look at ~을 또 사용해도 괜찮다.).

6. Introduce part 3 of the overview slide
목차 슬라이드 소개 (3)

아울러, ~에 대해서도 말씀드리겠습니다.

- **Then I'll show you** some data from a recent community health project.

Examples

- **Then I'll introduce** some data from a recent community health project.
- **Then I'll focus on** some data from a recent community health project.
- **After that I'll focus on** some data from a recent community health project.

그다음으로 넘어갈 때는 Then ~, After that ~ 등의 접속사를 사용한다.

7. Move on to the last part of the overview slide: Summary and future directions 목차 슬라이드의 마지막: 요약과 전망

마지막으로, 발표 내용을 요약한 후에 앞으로 남은 연구 과제에 대해 말씀드리겠습니다.

- **I'll finish with** a summary and **mention future directions.**

Examples

- **I'll summarize** the main points and **touch on** future studies / work / research.

The expressions **future directions**, **future plans** and **future studies** are plural. But **future work** and **future research** are singular and should not be in used in the plural form. You cannot say ***future works*** or ***future researches***. The expressions **future studies**, **future plans** and **future projects** are always plural in this context.

발표 끝부분에 요약과 전망을 제시한다.

'전망' 또는 '향후 연구 과제'라고 말할 때는 future studies, future plans, future projects 등은 반드시 복수형으로 표현하고, future work, future research는 반드시 단수형을 사용해야 하니 주의한다(203쪽 참고).

Common errors — 흔히 하는 실수

✕ This is *my* outline.
○ **This is an outline.**

You should avoid using ***my***. See page 16: Column, The word **my** is frequently misused.

My라는 단어를 사용할 때는 주의한다. 자세한 내용은 다음 쪽의 내용을 참고한다.

✕ This is ***today's*** topics.
○ **This slide shows the contents of my presentation.**

✕ This is ***today's*** contents.
○ **Here are the contents.**

Also avoid using the word ***today's***, as it is unnecessary. The words **presentation** and **talk** are more frequently used than **topic**. It is better to avoid the word **topic**.

'오늘의 발표'라고 말할 때 today's ~라고 말하지 않아야 한다. 또한, topic보다는 presentation 또는 talk 등의 단어를 사용하는 것이 좋다. 9쪽의 Common errors를 참고한다.

Column #01

The word my is frequently misused

My라는 표현을 함부로 쓰지 않도록 주의한다

Here are some common errors. In the following sentences, the use of the word my is unnatural and too informal.

✕ *This is my outline.*	◯ This is an outline.
✕ *This is my background.*	◯ This is some background.
✕ *Here are my contents.*	◯ These are the contents.
	◯ Here are the contents.
✕ *Here are my results.*	◯ Here are the results.
	◯ These are the results.
✕ *This is my summary.*	◯ This is a summary.
✕ *This is my conclusion.*	◯ This is the conclusion.
✕ *This is my apparatus.*	◯ This is the apparatus we used.
✕ *This is my hospital.*	◯ This is where I work.
✕ *This is my device.*	◯ This is the device we used.

However, please note the correct use of my in the following sentences.

◯ **My presentation today is about** + 2 or 3 words from the title.
◯ **My presentation is in 5 parts.**
◯ **This is my last slide.**

My라는 단어는 상대가 막역한 관계일 때 격식 없이 쓰는 표현이므로 정중한 학회 발표에서는 사용하지 않는 것이 좋다. 다만 my presentation이라고 표현하는 정도는 문제가 되지 않는다.

5 How to introduce an overview slide using the words first, next, then, after that, in part 3, in the next part / section, finally, lastly 목차 슬라이드를 소개할 때 사용할 수 있는 접속사 표현

5.1 How to emphasize the structure of the presentation 접속사 표현을 활용하여 발표의 구성을 강조하는 방법

When introducing an overview slide, some presenters emphasize the structure of the presentation using these words: **first**, **next**, **then**, **after that**, **in part 3**, **in the next part / section**, **finally**, **lastly**. Here is an example.

목차 슬라이드를 소개할 때, 왼쪽에 예시된 것처럼 순서를 구분하는 접속사 표현을 활용하여 발표의 전체적인 구성을 강조할 수 있다.

Script(접속사 표현을 활용하여 발표의 전체 구성을 명확하게 구분한 원고의 예)

Today, I want to focus on a new concept of treating Parkinson's disease. My presentation is in 5 main parts. First, I'll go over the main causes of the disease and treatments of the disease. Next, I'll explain the concept of atypical anti-Parkinson compounds. In part three, I'll discuss the effects of a prototype. After that, I'll consider animal models, namely monkeys. Finally, I'll focus on sites of action in the brain.

In the above example, the presenter introduces the topic with **focus on**. **Today, I want to focus on (topic)**. The number of sections in the presentation is introduced like this. **My presentation is in 5 main parts / has 5 parts / is divided into 5 parts / consists of 5 parts**. The following verbs are used to introduce the sections. **go over / explain / discuss / consider / focus on**.

'오늘 발표는 ㅇ개 부분으로 진행하겠습니다.'라고 말할 때는 **My Presentation is in 5 main parts** 등으로 표현한다.

5.2 How to introduce an overview slide using as few words as possible
목차 슬라이드를 더 간결하게 소개하는 방법

Some presenters avoid the words used in 5.1 above in order to save time and simplify the explanation. Instead they use the following verbs: **talk about**, **is**, **has**, **focus on**, **look at**, **mention**. Here is an example.

이전 쪽의 예시보다 접속사 표현을 줄여서 더 간결하게 표현하면 발표 시간을 절약할 수 있다.

Script(단어 수를 줄여 간결하게 표현한 원고의 예)

Today I am going to talk about standards. This is an outline. My presentation has 4 main parts. I'll focus on problems with standard measurement systems and look at ways of adapting them. I'll also look at performance. Finally, I'll look at reliability tests and show you some of the data we got. I'll also mention future work.

Note The presenter uses the two-word verb look at three times in this example. This saves time. This kind of repetition is not a problem in an oral presentation and is commonly used by native speakers. It is, of course, unacceptable in written academic English.

이 예시에서 look at ~이라는 표현을 여러 번 사용했는데, 이렇게 해도 구두발표에서는 문제가 되지 않는다. 하지만 문어체를 사용하는 학술 논문에서는 이렇게 하지 말아야 한다.

Key points

1. An overview slide will help the audience to understand the structure and contents of the presentation.
2. The key functions to use when introducing an overview slide are as follows:
   - **This is an overview/outline.**
   - **Here are the contents.**
   - **These are the points I'll be covering today.**
3. Introduce the structure of the presentation
   - **My presentation is in 5 parts.**
4. Refer to each part of the contents slide
   - **I'll start with an introduction.**
   - **I'll look at (topic).**
   - **I'll focus on (topic).**
   - **I'll move on to (topic).**
   - **I'll finish with a summary.**
5. Commonly used verbs for introducing the parts of an overview slide are as follows: start with, look at, focus on, move on to, finish with.
6. Some presenters use words such as first, next, then, after that, in part 3, in the next part / section, finally, lastly to introduce an overview slide. These help to indicate the structure of the presentation as clearly as possible.
7. Other presenters save time by using expressions such as talk about, is, has, focus on, look at and mention. Some native speakers use the word look at several times when introducing the slide. Repeating the same verb look at several times to introduce the material on the overview slide is not an issue.

• 발표 초반에 목차 슬라이드를 제시하면 청중이 발표의 전체 구성을 미리 파악할 수 있을 뿐 아니라 발표 내용도 쉽게 이해할 수 있다.

• 목차 슬라이드의 항목을 하나씩 소개해 갈 때는 look at ~ 또는 focus on ~ 등의 구동사(phrasal verb)를 활용하면 좋다. Look at ~ 등은 반복해서 사용할 수 있다.

• First, next 등의 순서를 나타내는 접속사 표현을 활용하면 좋다.

6 How to introduce an overview slide
목차 슬라이드를 소개하는 방법

Example 2: Here is an overview slide. The script is shown below.

Slide(목차 슬라이드의 예)

Role of iron plaque in controlling distribution and speciation of As and Cd in paddy soils

Overview

1. What is iron plaque?
2. Synchrotron micro-beam X-ray absorption
3. Distribution and speciation of As around iron plaque and iron mottle
4. Distribution and speciation of Cd around iron plaque
5. Conclusions and remaining questions

This is the supporting script to introduce the overview slide

Script(위의 목차 슬라이드를 소개하는 원고의 예)

① Thank you for the introduction. My name is Jane Stevens. I'm with the University of Oxford. ② Today I will focus on the role of iron plaque. ③ As you can see, my presentation has 5 parts. ④ First, I'll ask the question: What is iron plaque? ⑤ Next, I'll move on to synchrotron micro-beam X-ray absorption. ⑥ Then, I will look at distribution and speciation of As around iron plaque and iron mottle. ⑦ I will also look at distribution and speciation of Cd around iron plaque. ⑧ I'll finish with some conclusions ⑨ and briefly mention remaining questions. ⑩ I'll start by focusing on iron plaque.

Key sentences

1. Thank the chairperson 좌장에게 감사 인사를 한다

소개해주셔서 감사합니다.

- Thank you for the introduction.

Examples

- Thank you.
- Thank you, Chair.
- Thank you, Chairperson.
- Thank you, Professor Suzuki.
- Thank you for your kind introduction.

2. Introduce the topic 발표 주제를 소개한다

오늘은 ~에 대해서 발표하겠습니다.

- Today, I will focus on the role of iron plaque.

Examples

- Today, I'll talk about the role of iron plaque.
- Today, I want to look at the role of iron plaque.
- In this presentation, I'll be talking about the role of iron plaque.
- In this presentation, I'll be focusing on the role of iron plaque.

Note The patterns **I'll talk about** and **I'll be talking about** have the same meaning. The frequency of **I'll talk about** is much higher than **I'll be talking about.**

3. Refer to the structure of the presentation
발표의 전체 구성을 소개한다

오늘 발표는 ○개의 부분으로 나누어 진행하겠습니다.

- As you can see, **my presentation has 5 parts.**

Examples

- **My presentation is in 5 parts.**
- **This presentation is divided into 5 parts.**
- **There are 5 parts in this presentation.**
- **This presentation has 5 parts.**
- **This presentation consists of 5 parts.**

발표를 시작할 때 몇 부분으로 나누어 진행하는지 미리 알려 주면 청중이 전체 구성을 파악하기 쉽다.

4. Use a question to focus on the main topic
질문으로 발표 주제를 소개한다

먼저, 여러분께 질문을 드리겠습니다.

- **First, I'll ask the question**: What is iron plaque?

Examples

- **I'll start with the question**: What is iron plaque?
- I'd like to begin **by posing the question**: What is iron plaque?

Note The expression **to pose a question** is formal and means to ask a question.

'~란 무엇입니까?'와 같은 의문형으로 청중에게 질문을 던지면 발표 주제를 효과적으로 드러낼 수 있다.

5. Introduce the next section using the verb move on to

다음 주제로 넘어간다 (1)

다음으로, ~에 대해서 말씀드리겠습니다.

- **Next, I'll move on to** synchrotron micro-beam X-ray absorption.

Examples

- **Next, I'll go on to** synchrotron micro-beam X-ray absorption.
- **Next, I'll look at** synchrotron micro-beam X-ray absorption.
- **Next, I'll consider** synchrotron micro-beam X-ray absorption.
- **Next, I'll introduce** synchrotron micro-beam X-ray absorption.

목차 슬라이드의 다음 항목을 소개할 때는 왼쪽처럼 말하면 좋다.

6. Introduce the next section with the verb look at

다음 주제로 넘어간다 (2)

그리고 ~에 대해 말씀드리겠습니다.

- **Then I will look at** distribution and speciation of As around iron plaque and iron mottle.

Examples

- **Then I will focus on** distribution and speciation of As around iron plaque and iron mottle.
- **After that I will talk about** distribution and speciation of As around iron plaque and iron mottle.

목차 슬라이드의 각 항목을 말할 때는 **look at ~**, **focus on ~** 등의 구동사 표현을 활용하면 좋다.

7. Introduce the next section with the verb look at

다음 주제로 넘어간다 (3)

~에 대해서도 말씀드리겠습니다.

- I will also look at distribution and speciation of Cd around iron plaque.

Examples

- I will also discuss (topic).
- I will also consider (topic).

8. State how you will finish the presentation (1)

발표의 마지막 부분에 대해 말한다 (1)

마지막으로 요약하자면~ (9로 이어감)

- I'll finish with some conclusions (this sentence continues in 9. below).

Examples

- I'll conclude with a summary...
- Finally, I'll give a brief summary...

요약과 향후의 연구 과제를 언급하면서 목차 슬라이드의 소개를 마친다.

9. State how you will finish the presentation (2)

발표의 마지막 부분에 대해 말한다 (2)

~ 앞으로 수행할 연구 과제에 관해서도 말씀드리려고 합니다.

- ... and briefly mention remaining questions.

Examples

- ... and briefly touch on remaining questions.
- ... and talk about remaining issues.
- ... and say something about remaining issues.
- ... and mention future research.

앞으로 수행할 연구 과제에 대해 언급할 때는 mention ~, touch on ~ 등의 표현을 사용하는 경우가 많다.

The following verbs are useful for introducing future research, future work, future plans, remaining issues, applications: touch on, talk about, say something about, mention.

10. Start part one of the presentation

발표의 첫 번째 내용을 시작한다

그러면, 첫 번째로 ~에 관해 말씀드리겠습니다.

- I'll start by focusing on iron plaque.

Examples

- I'm going to start by talking about (topic).
- I'll start by looking at (topic).
- Let me start by describing (topic).

대략적인 구성을 알린 후에 발표의 본론으로 들어갈 때는 왼쪽 예시의 표현처럼 말하면 된다.

Note The grammar pattern, start / begin by + verb+ing (start by talking about / looking at / focusing on), is useful for introducing topics.

Key points

1. Introduce the structure of the presentation by stating the number of points, themes, topics you will cover.
   - **My presentation is in 5 parts.**
   - **My presentation has 5 parts / is divided into 5 parts / consists of 5 parts.**
2. Use a question to introduce / focus on an important topic.
   - **First, I'll ask the question: What is iron plaque?**
3. Indicate a new section/part of the presentation with the following expressions:
   - **Next, I'll move on to (topic).**
   - **Then I'll look at (topic).**
   - **After that, I'll mention (topic).**
   - **I'll also look at (topic).**

4. State how you will finish the presentation. I'll finish with a summary and mention future work.
   Useful verbs for stating how you will finish the presentation:
   - **I'll finish with / conclude with a summary.**

   Useful verbs for referring to future work:
   - **I'll mention / touch on / say something about future work.**
5. Start part one of the presentation
   - **I'll start / begin by focusing on / talking about (topic).**

• 발표를 시작할 때, 오늘의 발표가 몇 부분으로 이루어져 있는지 미리 언급하는 것이 좋다.

• 발표 주제를 소개할 때 의문형으로 청중에게 질문을 던지는 방법을 추천한다.

• 목차 슬라이드의 소개를 마친 후에는 I'll start by focusing on (topic) 등의 표현으로 본 주제로 들어간다.

7 How to show the title, your name, affiliation, and an overview of the contents on one slide
제목, 이름 · 소속, 목차를 한 장의 슬라이드로 소개하는 방법

Some presenters **combine slides 1 and 2**. This means that the **first slide will contain the title, your name, affiliation, and an overview of the contents.** The advantage is that the audience can scan the information in slide 1 as you are talking.

어떤 발표자는 발표 제목, 발표자의 이름 · 소속, 발표 목차 등을 슬라이드 한 장에 모두 담기도 한다. 이렇게 하면 청중에게 한 눈에 효율적으로 정보를 전달할 수 있다.

Here is an example.

Slide(제목 슬라이드와 목차 슬라이드를 한 장으로 묶은 예)

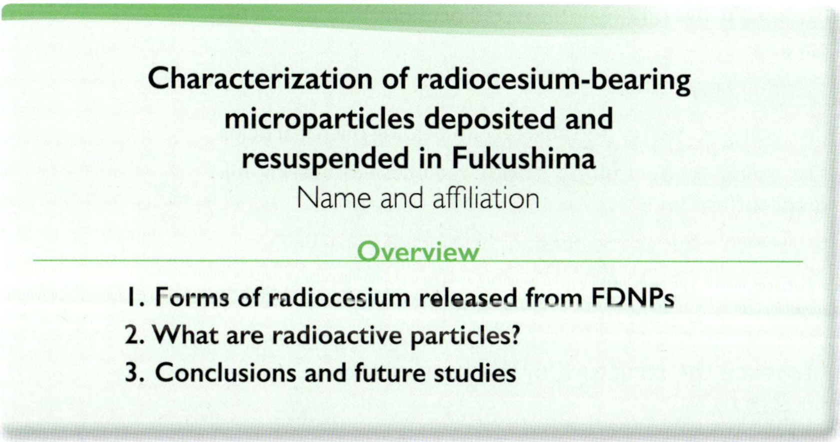

Script(위 슬라이드를 설명하기 위한 원고의 예)

① Thank you for the introduction. (Name and affiliation) ② Today I'll be talking about radiocesium bearing micro-particles. ③ Here are the contents. ④ I'll start by focusing on forms of radiocesium released from FDNPs. ⑤ Next, I'll ask the question: What are radioactive particles? ⑥ I'll finish with some conclusions and mention future studies.

Key sentences

1. Thank the chairperson 좌장에게 감사 인사를 한다

소개해주셔서 감사합니다.

- Thank you for the introduction.

Examples

- Thank you.
- Thank you for your kind introduction.

2. State the presentation topic 발표 주제를 소개한다

오늘은 ~에 관해 말씀드리겠습니다.

- Today I'll be talking about radiocesium bearing microparticles.

Examples

- I'm going to focus on radiocesium bearing microparticles.
- I'm going to be talking about radiocesium bearing microparticles.
- I want to look at radiocesium bearing microparticles.
- I'd like to talk about radiocesium bearing microparticles.

3. Introduce the structure of the presentation 목차 소개를 시작한다

목차를 소개하겠습니다.

- Here are the contents.

Examples

- Here / These are the contents.
- Here / These are the points / topics / things / areas I'm going to cover.
- These are the main points I'll cover today.

발표 주제를 소개한 다음에 목차 소개로 넘어갈 때는 왼쪽 같은 표현을 사용하면 좋다.

4. State the topic 목차 슬라이드의 각 항목에 대해 언급한다

첫 번째로 ~에 대해서 말씀드리겠습니다.

- I'll start by focusing on forms of radiocesium released from FDNPs

Examples

- I'll begin by looking at (topic).
- First, I'll look at (topic).
- In part I, I'll talk about (topic).

목차를 한 장의 슬라이드로 작성했을 때와 마찬가지로 목차의 각 항목을 차례로 소개한다.

5. Focus on a topic using a question

의문형으로 주제를 소개한다

다음으로, 여러분께 질문을 드리겠습니다.

- Next, I'll ask the question: What are radioactive particles?

Examples

- Next, I'll pose the question: What are radioactive particles?

의문형으로 청중에게 질문을 던짐으로써 발표할 주제를 인상적으로 부각할 수 있다.

6. State how you will finish the presentation

발표의 끝부분에 관해 언급한다

**마지막으로 앞의 내용을 요약하고,
향후의 연구 과제에 대해 말씀드리겠습니다.**

- I'll finish with some conclusions and mention future studies.

Examples

- I'll summarize the main points and touch on future research.
- I'll finish with a summary and talk briefly about our ongoing work.

"(자세한 내용은 언급하지 않고) 간단히 말씀드리겠습니다."라고 말할 때는 mention ~, touch on ~, talk briefly about ~ 등의 표현을 활용한다.

Key points

1. It is possible to save time by combining slides 1 and 2.
2. This means that the first slide shows the title, your name, affiliation and an overview of the contents.
3. Remember that the audience will rapidly scan the information on slide 1 as you are speaking.

발표 제목, 발표자의 이름과 소속, 발표 목차 등을 한 장의 슬라이드로 축약하면 청중이 대강의 발표 내용을 확인할 수 있어서 효율적으로 관련 정보를 전달할 수 있다.

8 Starting without an overview slide: a short overview that provides a snapshot of the topic
목차 슬라이드를 사용하지 않고 발표를 시작하는 방법

Some experienced presenters tell me that they do not generally use an overview slide. Instead, they give **a short oral overview** that **provides a snapshot** of the topic and contents. Here are the reasons they give. **There is not enough time. Everyone knows the material. The audience can follow the contents of the presentation without an overview slide.** I have included the following example for presenters who do not want to use an overview slide.

어떤 발표자들은 목차 슬라이드를 따로 만들지 않고 말로만 발표 내용을 설명하기도 한다. 이러한 방법은 목차 슬라이드를 소개할 시간이 부족하거나, 청중이 예비지식이 충분히 있는 경우, 목차 슬라이드가 없어도 청중이 발표 내용을 쉽게 이해할 수 있을 때 사용한다.

8.1 A short overview that provides a snapshot of the topic without using a slide
목차 슬라이드를 사용하지 않고 발표를 시작하는 방법 (1)

Example 1 (목차 슬라이드를 사용하지 않고 발표의 개략적인 내용을 설명하는 예 1)

Thank you for the introduction. My name is Susan Hastings. I'm with London University in the Department of Community Medicine. ① We have been working on ways of helping people at high risk of diabetes. ② Our main focus is community projects where pre-diabetic people meet with health workers in the community. ③ We are also interested in creating online support material for such people. ④ Currently, we are involved in a project monitoring the health of 1,500 high-risk individuals enrolled in community support projects.

⑤ Today I want to talk about community health interventions. ⑥ I'll start with some background. ⑦ Then I'll explain how community projects were set up, and talk about the research we conducted.

Key sentences

1. Statement of general research area 연구 영역에 관해 말한다

저희는 ○○(대략적인 연구 영역)에 관해 연구하고 있습니다.

- **We have been working on** ways of helping people at high risk of diabetes.

Examples

- We have been **doing research on** ways of helping people at high risk of diabetes.
- We have been **focusing on** ways of helping people at high risk of diabetes.
- We have been **looking at** ways of helping people at high risk of diabetes.
- We have been **investigating** ways of helping people at high risk of diabetes.

Note In example 1, the following pattern is used: **We have been doing research on + topic**. Please note that the following expression is grammatically incorrect: ***We are researching on (topic)***. The correct pattern is: **do + research on + topic**. Here are 2 examples.

- **We have been doing research on** (topic).
- **We are doing research on** (topic).

However, please note the following pattern. **We are researching the effect of sunlight on degradation rates**. The pattern is **to research the effect of X on Y**. The word **on** is also used in the following patterns. **This study was on** (topic). **This research was on** (topic). See p 74, Note We are studying *on*

먼저, 발표 배경의 하나로서 자신이 어떠한 연구를 하고 있는지 말한다.

연구 영역을 소개할 때는 We have been doing research on (+ topic)이라고 표현한다. *We are researching on (+ topic)*이라고 말하면 문법적으로 틀린 표현이다. 현재진행형으로 We are doing research on (+ topic) 또는 현재완료진행형으로 We have been doing research on (+ topic)이라고 말해야 한다.

전치사 on은 research on (+ topic) 외에 to research the effect of X on Y, 또는 This study was on (+ topic) 등의 표현에서도 활용한다.

2. Specific statement of topic 더 구체적으로 연구 주제를 소개한다

저희는 특히 ○○(구체적인 연구 주제)에 대해 연구하고 있습니다.

- Our main focus is community projects where pre-diabetic people meet with health workers in the community.

Examples

- We are looking at community projects where pre-diabetic people meet with health workers in the community.
- We are working on community projects where pre-diabetic people meet with health workers in the community.
- We are focusing on community projects where pre-diabetic people meet with health workers in the community.
- We are particularly interested in community projects where pre-diabetic people meet with health workers in the community.
- The main focus of our work is community projects where pre-diabetic people meet with health workers in the community.

대략적인 연구 영역을 설명한 후에 구체적인 내용을 부연하여 설명한다.

Note This is a short note on different patterns using the word focus. The example above uses the pattern, The main focus of our work is (+ topic).

The following patterns are also possible.

- The main focus of our work is on + topic.
- Our main focus is on + topic.
- Our main focus is + topic.
- We are focusing on + topic.

구체적인 연구 주제를 소개할 때는 focus ~라는 표현을 사용하는 것이 좋다. The main focus of our work is (+ topic)이라고 해도 되고, 왼쪽과 같은 표현도 활용할 수 있다.

3. Further statement of topic 연구 주제에 관해 좀더 언급한다

아울러, ~에 관련된 연구도 하고 있습니다.

- We are also interested in creating online support material for such people.

Examples

- Additionally, we are developing online support material for such people.
- In addition, we are making online support material for such people.

4. Statement of current research

현재의 연구 내용을 구체적으로 말한다

현재는 ~에 관한 연구를 진행하고 있습니다.

- (Currently), we are involved in a project monitoring the health of 1,500 high-risk individuals enrolled in community support projects.

Examples

- (Currently), we are developing a project monitoring the health of 1,500 high-risk individuals enrolled in community support projects.
- (At the moment), we are setting up a project monitoring the health of 1,500 high-risk individuals enrolled in community support projects.
- (Now,) we are creating a project monitoring the health of 1,500 high-risk individuals enrolled in community support projects.
- We are (now) creating a project monitoring the health of 1,500 high-risk individuals enrolled in community support projects.

연구 현황(어떤 프로젝트를 진행하고 있는지)을 소개한다. 왼쪽 예문 중에서 ( ) 안의 표현은 생략할 수 있다.

Note In the above examples, the words in parentheses can be omitted.

5. Introduce the presentation topic 발표 주제를 소개한다

오늘은 ~에 대해 발표하겠습니다.

- Today, I want to talk about community health interventions.

Examples

- Today, I am going to focus on community health interventions.
- Today, I want to consider community health interventions.
- Today, I'll be looking at community health interventions.
- My presentation is about community health interventions.
- My presentation is on community health interventions.

Note In the above preview, the title / topic of the presentation is introduced at the end of the short overview and not at the beginning. In function 5, the presenter introduces the topic of the presentation like this. Today, I want to talk about + topic. This means that in this type of overview, the position of the presentation title is flexible.

이 예시의 경우처럼, 발표 주제(타이틀)의 소개를 연구 내용에 대한 설명보다 나중에 하는 방식으로 응용할 수도 있다. 이처럼 발표 주제를 소개하는 시점을 융통성 있게 조정할 수 있다.

6. State that you will explain the background
연구 배경을 언급한다

우선, 연구 배경에 대해 말씀드리겠습니다.

- I'll start with some background.

Examples

- I'll give you some background.
- I'll explain the background.
- I'll mention some background.
- I'll start by explaining some background.

발표 주제를 소개한 후에 발표의 구성을 차례로 설명한다.

7. Introduce the next topic 다음으로 넘어간다

이어서, ~에 대해 말씀드리겠습니다.

- **Then I'll explain** how community projects were set up.

Examples

- After that **I'll tell you** how community projects were set up.
- Following that **I'll go over** how community projects were set up.

8.2 A short overview that provides a snapshot of the presentation without using a slide
목차 슬라이드를 사용하지 않고 발표를 시작하는 방법 (2)

Example 2(목차 슬라이드를 사용하지 않고 발표의 개략적인 내용을 설명하는 예 2)

Thank you. ① I'm Ken Williams. I'm with the University of Wales. I'm in the department of operative dentistry. ② Today I'll be talking about esthetic dentistry. ③ Over a number of years, we have been focusing on patient satisfaction levels. ④ We know that the number of people who want to improve the appearance of their teeth is increasing. ⑤ But we don't know much about levels of post-treatment patient satisfaction. ⑥ We looked at three commercial whitening products, ⑦ and focused on levels of patient satisfaction with those products. ⑧ We wanted to see how patients evaluated the products they used. ⑨ I'd like to start with some background.

Key sentences

1. Name and affiliation 이름과 소속

저는 ~대학의 ~라고 합니다.

- I'm Ken Williams. I'm with the University of Wales. I'm in the department of operative dentistry.

Examples

- I'm at the University of Wales. I'm in the department of operative dentistry.
- I'm working at the University of Wales. I'm in the department of operative dentistry.
- I work at the University of Wales. I'm in the department of operative dentistry.
- I'm with the University of Wales in the department of operative dentistry.

2. Introduce the topic 발표 주제의 소개

오늘은 ~에 대해 발표하겠습니다.

- Today I'll be talking about esthetic dentistry.

Examples

- I'm going to talk about esthetic dentistry.
- Today I'm going to focus on esthetic dentistry.

Note In this example, the presenter introduces the title/topic in function 2. In example 1, the title was introduced in function 5 (see page 35), which was later. This means that when giving a snapshot of the presentation, the position of the title/topic is flexible.

이 예시에서는 Example 1과 다르게 발표 수세를 가장 먼저 소개한다.

3. State the main research area 연구 영역에 대해 말한다

저희는 ~에 대해 연구하고 있습니다.

- Over a number of years, we have been focusing on patient satisfaction levels.

Examples

- Our main subject of interest is patient satisfaction levels.
- For several years, we have been looking at patient satisfaction levels.
- For a number of years, we have been working on patient satisfaction levels.

자신이 어떤 연구를 수행하고 있는지 설명한다. Over a number of years를 생략하고 좀더 간결하게 표현할 수도 있다.

Note It is possible to omit the following expressions: over a number of years, for several years, for a number of years. So, the shorter sentences without these expressions are as follows: We have been focusing on / We have been looking at / We have been working on + topic.

4. State the known information 이미 알려진 정보에 관해 언급한다

선행 연구에 따르면, ~인 것으로 밝혀졌습니다.

- We know that the number of people who want to improve the appearance of their teeth is increasing.

Examples

- A lot of groups have reported that the number of people who want to improve the appearance of their teeth is increasing.
- A lot of studies have reported that the number of people who want to improve the appearance of their teeth is increasing.
- It is well known that the number of people who want to improve the appearance of their teeth is increasing.
- It is well documented that the number of people who want to improve the appearance of their teeth is increasing.

'○○에 대해서는 잘 알려졌지만, △△에 대해서는 아직 모르는 것이 많습니다. 따라서 오늘은 △△에 대해서 ~'와 같은 표현으로 오늘 발표할 연구가 어떤 의의가 있는지 소개한다.

먼저, 선행 연구에서 어느 부분까지 밝혀졌는지 언급한다.

5. State the unknown information (This is known as the research gap/niche) 아직 연구가 이루어지지 않은 틈새(공백 부분)를 소개한다

하지만 ~에 대해서는 아직 잘 모르고 있습니다.

- **But we don't know much about** levels of post-treatment patient satisfaction.

Examples

- **However, we have no information on** levels of post-treatment patient satisfaction.
- **However, we have little information on** levels of post-treatment patient satisfaction.
- **However, there is little information on** levels of post-treatment patient satisfaction.
- **However, there is nothing on** levels of post-treatment patient satisfaction.
- **However, there are only a few studies on** levels of post-treatment patient satisfaction.
- **But, there is nothing in the literature on** levels of post-treatment patient satisfaction.
- **But, there is not much in the literature on** levels of post-treatment patient satisfaction.
- **However, there have been no reports in the literature on** levels of post-treatment patient satisfaction.
- **But, there have been few reports on** levels of post-treatment patient satisfaction.
- **However, few studies have focused on** levels of post-treatment patient satisfaction.

Note In all of the above examples, you can use either **however** or **but**.

Note For more information on the phrase **in the literature**, please see pages 67 and 166.

이어서 '아직 모르는 부분'을 소개한다.

'아직 모르는 부분'이란 표현은 **research gap** 또는 **research niche** 등의 용어를 사용한다.

However와 **But**는 어느 단어를 사용해도 상관없다.

In the literature의 사용법, 문헌/선행 연구에 관한 기타 표현에 대해서는 67쪽과 166쪽을 참고한다.

6. State research topic 1 연구 내용을 말한다 (1)

~을 조사했습니다.

- We looked at three commercial whitening products.

Examples

- We focused on three commercial whitening products.
- We investigated three commercial whitening products.
- We researched three commercial whitening products.
- We analyzed three commercial whitening products.

6~8에서는 구체적으로 어떤 연구를 어떤 목적으로 수행했는지 설명한다.

7. State research topic 2 연구 내용을 말한다 (2)

~에 대해서도 조사했습니다.

- We focused on levels of patient satisfaction.

Examples

- We concentrated on levels of patient satisfaction.
- We studied levels of patient satisfaction.

Note Any of the verbs in **6. State research topic 1** can also be used in **7. State research topic 2**.

8. State the objectives 연구의 목적을 말한다

이 연구의 목적은 ~입니다.

- We wanted to see how patients evaluated the products they used.

Examples

- Our objective was to find out how patients reacted to different products.
- The aim was to assess the patients' evaluation of particular products.

9. Introduce the background 연구 배경의 설명을 시작한다

그럼, 먼저 이 연구의 배경에 대해 말씀드리겠습니다.

- I'd like to start with some background.

Examples

- This is some background.
- Let's look at some background.
- I'll just run through some background.
- I'd like to show you some background.
- I'm going to show you the background.

발표 내용의 개요를 설명한 후에 연구 배경에 대한 설명으로 넘어갈 때는 왼쪽과 같은 표현을 사용한다.

Note The word background is usually singular and always one word.

In the above examples, there are two expressions: some background and the background. Both are possible.

Background는 단수형으로 표현하고, *back ground*로 띄어 쓰지 않도록 주의한다. some background와 the background 등은 모두 사용할 수 있다.

Key points

1. To save time, some presenters do not use an overview slide.
2. Instead, they give a short snapshot of the topic with no overview slide.
3. The material in 8. Pages 31～41 can be used to create a short snapshot with no overview slide. Some functions can be omitted, depending on the structure of your presentation and the time available.

- 목차 슬라이드를 사용하지 않고 발표를 시작할 수도 있다.
- 이런 경우에는 발표의 주제와 구성을 말로 간단하게 소개한다.

9 Introduce the background
연구 배경을 소개하는 방법

Presenters often include background information. This can vary from just a few sentences to several minutes of explanation with accompanying slides. In this section, I present key sentences for introducing background information.

발표의 주제와 구성을 설명한 후에 연구 배경을 소개한다.

연구 배경에 대한 소개는 2~3개 문장으로 간략히 끝낼 수도 있고, 슬라이드 몇 장을 준비해서 차근차근 설명할 수도 있다.

Script(연구 배경을 소개하기 위한 원고의 예)

① This is some background. ② There has been a lot of work on improving memory or slowing down memory loss in old people. ③ Most studies have focused on light exercise as a way of reducing risk of dementia. ④ We know that light physical exercise such as gardening, mild stretching and slow walking for periods of about ten minutes increases connectivity between parts of the brain associated with making and storing memory. While these studies have used various types of light exercise, ⑤ no studies have focused on the effectiveness of individual types of exercise. ⑥ One of the main goals of this study was to compare the effectiveness of the following 5 types of exercise: mild stretching, gardening, slow walking, tai chi and cooking.

Key sentences

1. Introducing the background to your research

연구 배경의 소개를 시작한다

지금부터 이 연구의 배경에 대해 말씀드리겠습니다.

- **This is some background.**

Examples

- **I'd like to start with** some background.
- **I'd like to mention** the background of/to this study.
- **I'd like to describe** the study background.
- **I'm going to run through** some background.
- **I want to go over** some background.

연구 배경에 대한 설명을 시작하겠다는 표현은 왼쪽의 예문처럼 한다.

The verbs **run through** and **go over** are used when you want to **focus only on the main points** and do not want to explain things in detail. The word **some** is usually used before **background**. Also, the word **background** in this context is **singular** and is one word. ***Back ground*** as two words is not correct.

상세히 다루지 않고 간단하게만 언급한다는 느낌을 전할 때는 구동사 **run through ~** 또는 **go over ~** 등의 표현을 활용한다. (57쪽 칼럼 참고)

Background는 하나의 단수형 단어로 사용하고, 두 단어로 나누어 ***Back ground***라고 하면 안 된다.

2. Referring to known information 선행 연구를 언급한다

~에 대해서는 지금까지 많은 연구가 진행되었습니다.

- **There has been a lot of work on** improving memory or slowing down memory loss in old people.

Examples

- **A lot of research has focused on** improving memory or slowing down memory loss in old people.
- As you know, **a lot of groups have been working on** improving memory or slowing down memory loss in old people.
- **There are several studies on** improving memory or slowing down memory loss in old people.

먼저, 관련된 선행 연구에 대해 언급한다.

Note In academic, written English, the above sentences would be as follows:

- Improving memory or slowing down memory loss in old people has received a lot of attention.
- Improving memory or slowing down memory loss in old people has attracted a lot of attention.
- A number of studies have addressed the issue of improving memory or slowing down memory loss in old people.

For an oral presentation, the patterns, **There has been a lot of work on / There are several studies on**, are more appropriate and easier to say.

선행 연구를 언급할 때 논문 등의 문어체 표현에서는 왼쪽처럼 하면 된다. 하지만 구어체로 발표할 때는 **There has been a lot of work on ~** 또는 **There are several studies on ~** 등의 표현을 사용한다.

3. Refer briefly to the studies mentioned in 2. Referring to known information

앞의 2에서 다룬 연구 내용을 간단히 소개한다

그간의 많은 연구에서는 ~에 대해 조사하였습니다.

- Most studies have focused on light exercise as a way of reducing risk of dementia.

Examples

- Most of these studies have looked at light exercise as a way of preventing memory loss.
- The majority of studies have looked at light exercise as a way of preventing memory loss.
- The vast majority of studies have looked at light exercise as a way of preventing memory loss.

This is an example of how to combine functions 1~3.

Script(1~3을 연결한 원고의 예)

I'd like to start with some background. There has been a lot of work on improving memory in people with mild dementia. Most studies have looked at light exercise as a way of preventing memory loss.

4. What is known and currently accepted in the field

해당 연구 영역에서 이미 밝혀진 부분에 대해 언급한다

현재 ~라는 것이 밝혀졌습니다.

- **Currently, we know that** light exercise is a good way of preventing memory loss.

Examples

- **We know that** light exercise is a good way of preventing memory loss.

Note In academic, written English, the above sentence would be as follows:

- It is known that light exercise is a good way of preventing memory loss.
- It is accepted that light exercise is a good way of preventing memory loss.
- It has been reported that light exercise is a good way of preventing memory loss.

For an oral presentation, the patterns, **Currently, we know that** and **We know that**, are more appropriate and also easier to say.

연구의 배경·목적을 설명할 때는 '선행 연구를 통해 ○○가 밝혀졌습니다.' → '그러나 △△에 대해서는 아직 잘 모르고 있습니다.' → '따라서 이 △△를 밝히기 위해 이 연구를 시행하였습니다.'라는 방식의 연결된 흐름으로 설명하는 것이 좋다. 먼저 **2, 3**에서 소개한 선행 연구의 결과로 무엇이 밝혀졌는지 간략하게 소개한다.

알려진 정보를 소개할 때 논문 등의 문어체 표현으로는 왼쪽처럼 하면 된다. 구어체로 발표할 때는 **Currently, we know that ~** 또는 **We know that ~** 등의 표현을 사용한다.

5. Research gap / niche 연구의 틈새(공백 부분)

The expression **research gap / research niche** refers to an area of research or an issue that has received little or no attention.

이어서, 아직 어떤 점이 알려지지 않았는지(연구의 틈새)를 설명한다.

하지만 ~에 주목한 연구는 아직 없습니다.

- No studies have focused on the benefits of light exercise on memory.

Examples

- There has been no work on the benefits of light exercise on memory.
- Few studies have focused on the benefits of light exercise on memory.
- Studies on the benefits of light exercise on memory have been limited to slow walking.

6. Research aims 연구의 목적

It is important to state the aims of the study. In this case, the presenter mentions the aims at the end of the background. Aims can also be referred to as **goals**, **objectives** and **motivation**.

이 연구는 ~하는 데에 목적을 두고 있습니다.

- One of the main goals of this study was to compare the effectiveness of the following 5 types of exercise: mild stretching, gardening, slow walking, tai chi and cooking.

Examples are divided into 4 groups as follows: goals, wanted, motivation and objectives.

연구의 목적을 소개할 때는 goals, wanted, motivation, objectives 등의 표현을 활용한다.

- Goals

  - One of the main goals of this study was to assess the potential benefits of light exercise.
  - These were the goals of this study: to assess the potential benefits of light exercise and to establish the most suitable forms of exercise.
  - One of our main goals was to assess the potential benefits of light exercise.
  - One of our long-term goals was to assess the potential benefits of light exercise.
  - Here are the goals: to assess the potential benefits of light exercise and to establish the most suitable forms of exercise.

- Wanted

  - We wanted to look at the potential benefits of light exercise.
  - We also wanted to look at the differences between the effectiveness of exercise types.

- Motivation

  - The main motivation of this study was to assess the potential benefits of light exercise.

- Objective

  - Our principle objective was to assess the potential benefits of light exercise.
  - Our main objective was to assess the potential benefits of light exercise.
  - The objective of this study was to assess the potential benefits of light exercise.

10 How to start a presentation as an invited speaker
초청 강연의 시작법

In this section, I introduce some useful sentences to use as an invited speaker.

Here is an example.

Script(초청 강연을 시작할 때의 원고 예시)

① Thank you very much for the introduction. ② Before I start, I'd like to say a big thank you to the organizers for inviting me. It is indeed a great honor to be here.

③ As you probably know, I'm a materials engineer. Currently, I'm at Imperial College, London in the Department of Engineering. ④ We are doing research on metal fatigue. ⑤ We are also interested in failure in other materials. ⑥ In recent years, we have been focusing on self-healing materials. ⑦ I'd like to start by giving a brief introduction to our work.

Key sentences

1. Thanking the chairperson 좌장에 대한 인사

소개해주셔서 감사합니다.

- Thank you very much for the introduction.

Examples

- Thank you, Dr. Watanabe, for introducing me.
- Thank you, Professor Williams, for that nice introduction. And thanks also to the rest of the committee for inviting me.
- Thanks, Bill, for introducing me.

일반적인 구두발표의 경우처럼, 가장 먼저 좌장에게 인사를 한다.

2. Thanking the organizers 학회 주최자, 실행위원 등에 대한 인사

이런 귀한 기회를 주셔서 감사드립니다.

- Before I start, I'd like to say a big thank you to the organizers for inviting me.

좌장에게 인사를 한 후, 학회 주최자와 실행위원 등의 관계자에게 초청 강연의 자리를 마련해 준 것에 대해 감사를 표한다.

Examples

- I'd like to say that it is a great pleasure and an honor to be invited to speak here today.
- I must say that it is a great honor to present at this conference. I would very much like to thank the organizers, particularly Dr. Suzuki from Tokyo University, who has made all the arrangements for my trip.
- Thank you very much indeed for this kind invitation. It is indeed a great honor to be here.
- Thank you very much for giving me the opportunity to speak at this conference.

3. Background 소속, 연구 영역 등의 소개

저는 ~의 분야에서 연구하고 있습니다.

- As you probably know, I'm a materials engineer.

자기소개로 직업, 소속, 연구 영역 등을 밝힌다.

Examples

- I'm a materials engineer.
- My background is in materials engineering.
- I have a background in materials engineering.
- I'd just like to mention my background and current research.
- I'm a medical doctor and have a background in community health.
- Basically, I am an environmental engineer. My main interest is in building materials. In other words, composite materials used in construction. For example, concrete.

- So, I'm at Imperial College, London in the Department of Engineering. As you probably know, we are working on self-healing construction materials, particularly concrete.
- Currently, I'm at Imperial College, London in the Department of Engineering.

4. Research interests 1 연구 내용에 대한 설명 (1)

주로 ~에 대해 연구하고 있습니다.

- We are doing research on metal fatigue.

Examples

- My main research interest is metal fatigue.
- Our main research focus is on metal fatigue.

4~6에서는 일반적인 구두 발표와 마찬가지로 자신이 어떤 연구를 하고 있는지 간략하게 설명한다.

5. Research interests 2 연구 내용에 대한 설명 (2)

아울러, ~에 대해서도 연구하고 있습니다.

- We are also interested in failure in other materials.

6. Current research 현재 진행하고 있는 연구 과제의 소개

최근에는 주로 ~의 주제에 관해 연구를 진행하고 있습니다.

- In recent years, we have been focusing on self-healing materials.

Examples

- Right now, we are working on (topic).

7. Starting 강연의 개시

그럼 첫 번째로 ~에 대해서 말씀드리겠습니다.

- **I'd like to start by giving a brief introduction to our work.**

Examples

- **I'll start by talking about** (topic).
- **I'd like to start with some background.**
- **I'll spend the first 5 minutes of my presentation talking about** (topic).

인사와 자기소개를 마치고 강연 주제로 들어갈 때는 왼쪽처럼 말한다.

11 Useful sentences for: Thanking the audience for coming, Making informal opening comments, Giving a series of talks, Comments when you present after a well-known presenter, Dealing with technical problems 편리한 표현 모음

In this section, I include a variety of useful sentences that do not fit in the categories already covered in this section.

11.1 Thanking the audience 청중에 대한 인사

At conferences where there are multiple, simultaneous sessions, some presenters start by thanking the audience for attending. Here are some examples.

1. Thanking people for coming to your presentation
자신의 발표에 참석해 준 청중에게 감사 인사

- Thank you for coming today.
- Thank you very much for coming today.
- Before I start, I'd just like to say thank you for coming today.

2. Thanking attendees for attending a session scheduled late in the day or at the end of a conference 최종 연제 또는 마지막 날 발표에 참석해 준 청중에게 감사 인사

- This is the last presentation slot today. So, thank you very much for coming.
- It's the last day of the conference. I'd like to thank you for sticking around and coming to this presentation.
- This is the last day of the conference and also the last session. I must say that I'm very pleased to see so many people. Thank you for coming.

11.2 Informal opening comments
발표를 시작할 때 사용하는 격식 없는 인사 방법

At an informal presentation, you may want to make some opening comments.

- It's great to see so many people here. Thank you for coming.
- There are just a few people here today, so please feel free to ask questions whenever you like.

11.3 Useful sentences for when you are giving a series of talks
여러 날에 걸쳐 이어지는 강연을 할 때 사용하는 표현

If you are giving a series of talks over a number of days or weeks, possibly as a visiting professor, or several presentations at the same conference, the following sentences may be useful.

1. Refer to previous presentations 지난번 내용의 복습

- My last talk focused on theoretical approaches. This evening I'll be talking about applications and our ongoing research work.
- Previously, I spoke about self-healing materials, particularly paint. Today, I want to talk about (topic).
- Last week, I spoke about / focused on self-healing materials, particularly paint. This presentation is on (topic).
- So, in my last lecture I was talking about self-healing materials, particularly paint. Today, I will be covering (topic).
- I can see some people here who were at my presentation in Korea last week. I'd just like to say that I'm going to cover some of the same ground, but I'll also be focusing on pain and the temporomandibular joint. So, you will have heard some of this before, but the majority of what I have to say is new.

2. Refer to future presentations 다음 강연 내용의 예고

- I'd just like to mention that I have one more presentation on Tuesday. It's on (topic). If you are interested, please come along. It would be great to see you.
- I have one more talk next week, which will be on (topic). That will be my last talk.
- Next week, I'll be talking about (topic).
- I'll be covering (topic) in the next presentation, which is on Friday.

11.4 Comments when you present after a well-known presenter
저명한 강연자의 바로 다음 순서로 발표할 경우의 발언

In some cases, you will need to present after a well-known presenter. Here are some useful sentences that are divided into 2 steps. In step 1, you can make a short comment on the previous presentation. In step 2, you start your presentation.

Step 1 앞 강연자의 발표에 대해 언급한다.

- It is a difficult task to speak after Dr. Williams' wonderful presentation.
- It is not easy to speak after such an impressive presentation.
- I think that Dr. Williams has just about said everything there is to say about (topic).
- After Dr. Williams' wonderful presentation, there is not much left for me to say.

Step 2 자기 발표를 시작한다

- However, I have some recent data that I hope will be of interest to you. So, I'd like to get started.
- However, it is possible that some of the material I'm covering today will fit in nicely with Dr. Williams' presentation.

11.5 Dealing with technical problems
컴퓨터, 프로젝터 등의 기기에 문제가 생겼을 때의 대응

Most presenters will have experienced some kind of technical problems with computers, projectors and so on. Here are some useful sentences to use in those situations.

1. Apologizing for a technical problem at the beginning of the presentation
발표 초기에 문제가 발생했을 때

- Sorry about the technical problems.
- I'm afraid we are having some technical problems.
- I'm afraid we are having some problems with this computer / system / projector.

2. After the problem has been solved 문제를 해결한 후의 표현

- Sorry to have kept you waiting.
- I think we can get started now.
- Ok. I think we are ready to start now.

3. Apologizing for problems that occur in the middle of the presentation
발표 도중에 문제가 생겼을 때

Sometimes problems may occur in the middle of your presentation. Here are some useful sentences.

- Sorry about that. I had an issue with some software / this computer / a video clip.
- We are having problems with the connection. Just a moment. Okay, we have fixed that. I'd like to continue.

4. When something such as a video clip or animation does not work
동영상이 중간에 멈추거나 아예 나오지 않는 등의 문제가 생겼을 때

- **We're having trouble with** the computer / the sound system / an adaptor.
- **There's an issue with** the computer / the sound system / an adaptor.
- **I had hoped to** show you a video clip. **But that doesn't seem to be possible. I'd like to move on to** the next section.
- **I had a brief video clip I wanted to show you**, **but it doesn't seem to be working**. **So I'll skip that**.
- **I wanted to show you** a video clip of the reaction, **but I have had a technical issue**.
- **I'll have to skip the video**. **Sorry about that**. / **I apologize for that**.

Column #02

I'll just run through / go over the main points

Run through ~, go over ~ 등의 표현을 잘 사용하자

The expressions **run through** and **go over** signal to the audience that you will concentrate on the most important information on a slide.

- I'll just run through the main points.
- There is a lot of data here. I'll run through the most important results.
- I'll just go over the important data.
- There is a lot of data here. I'll go over the main points.

It is highly likely that some of your slides are going to be busy and, on some occasions, you will have to skip some material. This is exactly when the expressions **run through** and **go over** will be useful.

"상세한 부분까지는 다루지 않고 핵심적인 내용만 간단히 언급하겠습니다."라고 말할 때는 run through ~ 또는 go over ~ 등이 가장 적절한 표현이다.

Part 2

Using informal, spoken English to simplify and shorten the main body

구어체 영어로 간결하게 구두발표용 원고를 작성하는 방법

In this section, I provide examples of **how to change formal English to informal English**. Each example has a formal sentence and examples in informal English.

구두발표에서 사용하는 '구어체'의 영어는 논문에서 사용하는 '문어체'의 영어와 차이가 있다. 구두발표용 원고에 논문의 문장을 그대로 사용한다면 이는 말로 옮기기에 적합하지 않아 지루하고 딱딱한 느낌을 준다. 이 장에서는 여러 예시를 바탕으로 논문에서 쓰는 문어체 영어를 발표에서 사용하는 구어체 영어로 바꾸는 방법을 소개한다.

1 How to reduce the level of formality in your presentation
문어체 영어를 구어체 영어로 바꾸는 방법

Note The example sentences presented in this section are for oral presentations and are generally too informal for use in an academic paper.

이 장에서 소개하는 예문은 모두 구두발표에서만 사용하는 구어체의 영어이다. 따라서 이를 논문 작성 시에 사용하는 것은 적절하지 않으니 유의하기 바란다.

Let's start by looking at a typical example of written academic English.

아래 내용에서 문어체 문장은 회색 사각형으로, 이를 구어체 영어로 고친 예문은 녹색 네모로 구분하였다.

- The receptor has been shown to play an important role in the mechanism.

↓

1. **We know that the receptor has an important role in the mechanism.**
2. **The receptor has an important role in the mechanism.**
3. **The receptor is important in terms of the mechanism.**

원래 문장은 수동태이지만 1~3은 모두 능동태의 표현으로 바꿨다.

'~에 관하여', '~에 있어서'라고 말할 때는 3처럼 in terms of ~를 사용한다.

Here are some examples of how to reduce the formality of this sentence.
You will notice that example 1 starts with **we** and is **active** not **passive**. The verb **shown to play** has been deleted. Examples 2 and 3 are also in the active tense. Sentence 3 uses the useful expression **in terms of**. Examples 1 ~ 3 are much shorter and less formal than the original.

- This lipid is expected to be used as a detergent and a lubricant.

1. **We think that** this lipid can be used as a detergent or lubricant.
2. **This lipid can probably be used as** a detergent or lubricant.

1은 **is expected to** ~를 **We think that** ~으로 대체하였다.

2는 **probably**라는 단어를 사용하여 확신 정도를 약하게 표현하고 있다.

The formality has been reduced by changing the expression **is expected to** to **we think that**. In example 2, the strength of the statement has been reduced by using the expression **can probably be used as**.

- These systems are expected to have applications in the medical field.

1. **We think** these systems have medical applications.
2. **These systems have** medical applications.

원래 문장은 수동태이지만, 1은 **We think** ~로 시작하는 능동태 표현이다.

Example 1 is an active sentence starting with **we**, using the word **think** instead of **expected**. In example 2, **we think** has been omitted. **These systems have medical applications**. Example 2 is more direct and stronger in tone than **These systems are expected to have applications in the medical field**. The original sentence has eleven words. Example 2 has only five words. The original sentence is too formal for an oral presentation.

2와 같이 **We think** ~라는 표현을 쓰지 않으면 확신 정도를 강하게 드러낼 수 있다.

이런 방식으로 구어체 영어로 바꾸면 글자 수를 원래 문장의 11개 단어에서 1은 7개 단어, 2는 5개 단어로 각각 줄일 수 있어서, 시간제한이 있는 구두 발표에서 간결하게 말할 수 있는 장점이 있다.

- It is suggested that the difference is caused by plastic deformation.

↓

1. **We think that the difference is caused** by plastic deformation.
2. **This difference is caused by** plastic deformation.
3. **The difference is due to** plastic deformation.
4. **The difference is probably caused by** plastic deformation.

It is suggested ~는 논문에서 사용하는 문어체의 표현이므로 삭제한다.

It is suggested ~처럼 확신 정도를 약하게 표현하고 싶다면 1, 4와 같이 We think ~ 또는 probably를 사용한다. 확신 정도를 강하게 표현할 때는 2, 3과 같이 단정적으로 말한다.

The phrase **It is suggested that** has been deleted because it is too formal for a presentation. The meaning of **It is suggested** is expressed by the phrases **We think that** or **The difference is probably caused by**. The word **probably** in example 4 is used to **tone down the strength of the sentence**.

Note The phrase **It is suggested that** is weaker than **The difference is due to**.

In an oral presentation, it is acceptable to use strong statements such as **the difference is due to**. In a written paper, however, it might be necessary to **tone down the strength of your statement** by using expressions like **It is suggested that / It is thought that / It is considered that**. While these expressions are used in written English, they are not commonly used in oral presentations.

일반적으로 구두발표에서는 논문과 달리 단정적인 표현도 사용할 수 있다. 이에 비해 논문 작성 시에 단정할 만한 근거가 없는 경우에는 It is suggested that ~, It is thought that ~, It is considered that ~ 등의 문장으로 확신 정도를 약하게 표현한다.

- From the present data, it is thought that reliability increases by about 20 percent.

↓

1. **As the data shows, there is an increase in** reliability of about 20 percent.
2. **As the data shows, reliability increases by about** 20 percent.
3. **These results/data indicate** that there is an increase in reliability of about 20 percent.
4. **These results/data show an increase in** reliability of about 20 percent.
5. **There is an increase in** reliability of about 20 percent.
6. **So, this means that** there is an increase in reliability of about 20 percent.

'보여 드린 데이터를 통해 ~라는 것을 알 수 있습니다'라고 말할 때 논문에서는 **from the present data**라는 문장으로 작성하지만, 말로 하는 구두발표에서는 간단하게 **As the data shows ~**, **The results/data indicate ~**, **So ~, this means that ~** 등으로 언급한다.

'데이터를 통해 ~'라는 표현을 생략하고 **5**와 같이 말해도 된다.

Increase 뒤에 오는 전치사는 **in**을 써야 하니 주의한다.

The phrase **from the present data** has been deleted because it is unnecessary. The expression, **it is thought that** has also been deleted. In example 6, the phrase **So, this means that** refers to the data that has been presented. The shortest sentence is 5., which uses the simple pattern, **There is an increase in** reliability of about 20 percent. Please note the preposition **in** after the word increase.

- Earthquakes are categorized into 3 types.

↓

1. **There are 3 types of** earthquakes.

The sentence pattern has been changed and the word **categorized** deleted. Example 1 starts with **there**. The revised sentence is much easier to say.

'~ 종류로 분류된다'라는 수동태 표현을 '~ 가지 종류가 있다'라는 능동태 표현으로 바꾸어 말할 수 있다. **Categorized**를 삭제하여 간단한 문장으로 고치면 발음하기도 쉽다.

- It is anticipated / expected / predicted / thought / suggested that the intensity of typhoons will increase in the future.

↓

1. **We think that** the intensity of typhoons will increase in the future.
2. **This data suggests that** typhoons will become stronger in the future.
3. **Typhoons will probably increase** in intensity in the future.
4. **It is quite likely / highly likely** that typhoons will increase in intensity in the future.
5. **We think that** typhoons will get stronger.

The verbs **anticipated**, **expected**, **predicted**, **thought**, **suggested** have been deleted as they are more suitable for academic papers. Example 1 is active and uses the phrase **We think that**. Example 3 uses simple grammar: **Typhoons will probably increase in intensity in the future**. In example 4, the strength of the sentence can be varied by using the expressions **quite likely**, **highly likely**. Sentence 5 is the shortest and only has seven words. **Get stronger** is an informal expression that means **increase in intensity**.

> **Note** It is better to avoid sentences patterns like these in your presentations: **It is anticipated / expected / predicted / thought / concluded / suggested that**. These expressions are more suitable for written English.

It is anticipated / expected / predicted / thought / suggested ~ 등은 논문 작성에 사용하는 문어체 표현이므로 구두발표에서는 피하는 것이 좋다.

4에서는 **quite likely**, **highly likely** 등의 표현으로 확신 정도를 높여서 말한다.

5에서는 **increase in intensity**(강도가 증가한다)를 **get stronger**라고 바꾸어 말하고 있다.

- The device does not have any faults.

↓

1. **The device has no faults.**
2. **There are no faults.**

In this example, it is possible to reduce the number of words from seven to four.

원래 문장은 '결함이 없다'를 **does not have any faults**라고 했는데, 이를 **has no faults** 또는 **There are no faults**로 바꿔서 간결하게 말할 수 있다.

- It has been reported that online interventions in the form of questionnaires and reminders can help at risk people to control their weight.

↓

1. **We know that** online interventions in the form of questionnaires and reminders can help people to control their weight.

The expression **It has been reported that** is commonly found in written academic English. In oral presentations, a short, simple expression is **We know that.**
See page 38 for more information on how to refer to other data.

It has been reported that ~은 이미 알려진 정보를 언급할 때 논문에서 자주 사용하는 표현이지만, 구두발표에서는 간결하게 **We know that** ~이라고 말하는 것이 좋다.

- We succeeded in fabricating new materials.

↓

1. **We were able to make** new materials.
2. **We were able to produce** new materials.
3. **We managed to make** new materials.
4. **We managed to produce** new materials.
5. **We made** new materials.
6. **We produced** new materials.

The expression **succeeded in fabricating** is quite formal and grammatically complex. It stresses the difficulty of doing something. Here are some examples with easier expressions using **were able to**, **managed to**, **made**, **produced**.
The simplest sentences are as follows: **We made** and **We produced**. Unless there is a specific need to stress that production was difficult to achieve, it is better to use **made** or **produced** in the simple past tense than **we succeeded in + verb + ing**.

'~ 하는 데 성공했다'를 **succeeded in ~ ing**이라고 표현하는 것은 논문에서 쓰는 딱딱한 문어체이다. 구어체로 '~을 이뤄냈다'라는 느낌을 표현하려면 **managed to (+ make/produce)** 를 사용하고, 그럴 필요가 없는 경우는 **5, 6**과 같이 단순히 '~했다'는 식으로 말한다.

- Epicenters have received a lot of attention.
- Epicenters have attracted a lot of attention.

The expressions **have received a lot of attention / have attracted a lot of attention** are commonly found in the introduction sections of academic papers. Here are some less formal examples commonly used in oral presentations.

↓

1. A lot of people **are working on** epicenters.
2. A lot of people **are doing research on** epicenters.
3. A lot of people **are focusing on** epicenters.
4. **There has been a lot of research on** epicenters.
5. **There has been a lot of work on** epicenters.
6. Epicenters **are an important topic**.
7. Epicenters **are a hot topic**.

In examples 1-3, the informal verbs **work on**, **do research on**, **focus on** are used. In examples 4 and 5, the words **research** and **work** are nouns that take the preposition **on**. Common patterns are **a lot of research on** and **a lot of work on**. Examples 6 and 7 use the verb **are** in the patterns, **are an important topic**, **are a hot topic**.

선행 연구에 대해 '~에 관한 연구는 많다'라고 말할 때 논문에서는 **have received a lot of attention, have attracted a lot of attention** 등의 수동태 문장으로 작성하지만, 구두 발표에서는 '많은 사람이 ~에 대해 연구하고 있다'(1~3), '~에 관한 연구는 많다'(4, 5), '~는 많은 연구자들이 주목하는 주제이다'(6, 7) 등의 능동태로 말한다.

1~3에서는 구어체에서 자주 사용하는 구동사 **work on ~, do research on ~, focus on ~** 등을 활용하여 말하고 있다.

4, 5에서는 **research, work**를 명사로 사용하고 있다. 이 단어 뒤에 오는 전치사는 모두 **on**을 붙이니 주의해야 한다.

6, 7에서는 연구자가 관심을 두는 부분이라는 표현을 **are an important topic, are a hot topic** 등의 방식으로 말한다.

- In the literature, there are few reports on adhesives suitable for this kind of restoration.

1. **There are few reports on** adhesives suitable for this kind of restoration.
2. **No studies have focused on** adhesives suitable for this kind of restoration.
3. **There is not much data on** adhesives suitable for this kind of restoration.
4. **There are few people working on** adhesives suitable for this kind of restoration.
5. **Few people are working on** adhesives suitable for this kind of restoration.
6. **There has not been much work on** adhesives suitable for this kind of restoration.
7. **There has not been any work on** adhesives suitable for this kind of restoration.

앞쪽의 예시와는 반대로, '~에 관한 연구는 적다'라고 말할 때는 왼쪽처럼 표현한다.

The above sentence, **In the literature, there are few reports on** (topic) is grammatically correct, but the use of the expression **in the literature** makes it quite formal. The examples 1~7 show simpler sentences with the same meaning that do not use **in the literature**. For examples of how to use the expression **in the literature** correctly, please see page 166.

In the literature라는 표현은 논문 같은 느낌을 주므로 구두발표에서는 사용하지 않는 것이 좋다. 그 사용법에 대해서는 166쪽을 참고한다.

- Candidates were assigned to 3 groups.

↓

1. We divided candidates into 3 groups.
2. We put candidates into 3 groups.
3. We assigned candidates to 3 groups.

The sentence has been changed from passive to active. In examples 1 and 2, the formal verb **assigned** has been changed to **divided into** or **put into**. **Assigned** is the most formal verb and **put** is the most informal verb. Assigned is used in example 3 in an active sentence.

'대상자를 ○개의 군으로 할당했다'고 말할 때 **assign**을 수동태를 쓰는 것은 논문식 표현이다. 따라서 구어체로는 **We divided ~ into ~ groups** 또는 **We put ~ into ~ groups**라고 말한다. **Assign**이라는 용어를 쓸 때도 능동태로 표현한다.

- Novel devices are being intensively studied to solve the problem of energy consumption.

↓

1. **A lot of people are working on** new devices to solve the problem of energy consumption.
2. **A lot of people are looking at** new devices to solve the problem of energy consumption.
3. **A lot of people are doing research on** new devices to solve the problem of energy consumption.
4. **Several groups are doing research on** new devices to solve the problem of energy consumption.
5. **Many researchers are working on** new devices to solve the problem of energy consumption.

The original sentence looks as if it has been copied from the introduction of an academic paper. It is too formal for an oral presentation. The verb **studied** has been changed to **working on, looking at**, and **doing research on**. The examples are active.

'~는 집중적으로 연구되고 있다'(**are being intensively studied**)는 논문식 표현이므로, '많은 사람이 ~에 대해 연구하고 있다'로 바꿔서 능동태의 현재진행형 문장으로 말한다. '연구하다'를 뜻하는 동사도 study가 아니라 **work on ~, look at ~, do research on ~** 등의 용어를 사용한다.

- These results strongly suggest that adhesion is at lower levels than previously reported.

1. **So, this means that** adhesion is at lower levels **than previously reported**.
2. **This means that** adhesion is at lower levels **than previously reported.**
3. **Adhesion is at** lower levels **than previously reported**.
4. **Adhesion is at** lower levels **than we previously thought**.
5. **Adhesion is at** lower levels **than we thought**.

'이 결과는 ~'라고 말할 때 구어체로는 (So) **this means that** ~이라고 하면 좋다. 3~5와 같이 이 부분을 생략하고 간결하게 말할 수도 있다.

'이전에 보고된 것보다' 또는 '이전에 생각했던 것보다'라고 말할 때는 ~ **than previously reported**라는 표현보다 구어체로 ~ **than we (previously) thought**라고 할 수도 있다.

The expression **These results strongly suggest that** is formal. Examples 1 and 2 use less formal expressions, **So this means that** and **This means that**, both of which refer to the results that have just been presented. The sentence can be shortened by deleting **These results strongly suggest that**. In examples 4 and 5, **than previously reported** has been changed to more informal expressions **than we previously thought** and **than we thought**. Example 5 has eight words whereas the original sentence has thirteen.

- The system is under development.

1. **The system is being developed.**
2. **We are (currently) developing** the system.
3. **We are (currently) working on** the system.

원래 문장에서는 '~를 개발 중이다'를 ~ **under development**라고 썼지만, 1~3은 모두 현재진행형으로 바꿔서 말하고 있다. 2, 3의 **currently**는 생략해도 된다.

In examples 2 and 3, the word **we** is used with the verbs **developing** and **working on**. If necessary, the word **currently** can be deleted.

- From these results, it was concluded that reliability increased.

↓

1. **These results show** that reliability increased.
2. **As you can see,** reliability increased.
3. **Reliability increased.**

'이상의 결과로부터 ~와 같이 결론을 내릴 수 있다'는 표현은 논문에서는 From these results, it was concluded ~라고 쓰지만, 구어체로는 1~3처럼 간결하게 말하는 것이 좋다.

The expression **it was concluded that** is commonly found in academic papers and is too formal for oral presentations. The three examples are much simpler, shorter and easier to say. They have been changed from passive to active. The expression **from these results** is unnecessary and has been deleted.

- A significant increase in values was observed in group 1.

↓

1. **We found that** values increased significantly in group 1.
2. **There was a** significant increase in values in group 1.
3. **Values increased** significantly in group 1.
4. **Values increased a lot** in group 1.
5. **Group 1 values** increased a lot.

'~가 관찰되었다/보였다'라는 표현은 논문에서는 수동태로 was observed가 되지만, 구어체로는 We found ~ 또는 There was ~와 같이 능동태로 말한다. 이 부분을 생략하고 3~5처럼 간결하게 말할 수도 있다.

The sentence has been changed from passive to active and starts with **we found** or **there was**. It is also possible to omit **we found** and **there was**, and start the sentence with the word **values**. For example, 3. **Values increased significantly in group 1** and 4. **Values increased a lot in group 1**. Example 5, **Group 1 values increased a lot** is the shortest.

- Furthermore, reliability was analyzed.

1. **We also looked at** reliability.
2. **We also focused on** reliability.
3. **We also analyzed** reliability.
4. **In addition, we analyzed** reliability.

Furthermore, reliability was analyzed is an example of written scientific English using the passive and a formal verb **analyzed**. The sentence has been changed from passive to active, and the word **furthermore** has been changed to **also** or **in addition**. The informal two-word verbs **look at** and **focus on** have been used instead of the more formal **was analyzed**. In examples 3 and 4, **analyzed** is used in an active sentence using **we**.

'~에 대해 조사했다'고 말할 때 **analyze**를 수동태로 하면 논문식 표현이 되므로, 구어에서는 능동태로 look at ~ 또는 focus on ~ 등의 구동사를 활용하는 것이 좋다.

'더욱이 ~'는 **furthermore**보다 **also** 또는 **in addition** 등의 표현이 구어체로 적합하다.

- In the present study, a new simulation method was employed.

1. **We used** a new simulation method.
2. A new simulation method **was used**.

The expression **in the present study** is redundant and should be deleted because it is obvious that you are talking about your current research and not some other research. The word **employed** has been changed to **used**. The expression **in the present study** is generally only used when you are talking about a series of studies and relating them to each other. Example 1 is active and example 2 is passive.

'이 연구에서는 ~라는 방법을 이용했다'고 말할 때 '이 연구에서는'(**in the present study**) 부분은 굳이 언급하지 않아도 되므로 구두발표에서는 생략한다. 또한, 논문에서는 '(방법을) 사용한다'라는 뜻의 동사를 **employ**로 쓰지만, 구두발표에서는 쉬운 용어인 **use**로 말한다.

- The level must not be in excess of 20 percent.
- The level must not exceed 20 percent.

↓

1. **The level must not be more than** 20 percent.
2. **The level should not be more than** 20 percent.

논문에서는 '초과하다'는 표현을 be in excess of ~ 또는 exceed ~라고 하지만, 말로 구두발표를 할 때는 be more than ~이라고 하면 된다.

The formality of the expressions **must not be in excess of** and **must not exceed** should be reduced. **In excess of** and **exceed** can be changed to **must not be more than** or **should not be more than**.

- The system can be applied in a variety of industries such as construction.

↓

1. **We can use this system** in industries such as construction.
2. **You can use this system** in industries such as construction.
3. **This system can be used in** industries such as construction.
4. **This system can be used in** construction.

원래 문장은 수동태인 can be applied로 되어 있으나, 1, 2에서는 We (You) can use로 시작하는 능동태의 문장이다. 이 경우에 We 또는 You 어느 쪽을 사용해도 괜찮다.

1~4 모두는 원래 문장의 a variety of ~를 생략하여 글자 수를 줄였다. 4는 industries such as ~도 생략하였다.

In examples 1 and 2, the sentence structure has been changed from passive to active. The word **applied** has been changed to **you can use**. Please note that **you** and **we** can both be used. In the last example, **industries such as** has been deleted and the sentence starts with the expression: **This system can be used in** (construction).

- The mechanism has not been elucidated.
- The mechanism is unknown.
- The mechanism is not fully understood.

The above three sentences have the same meaning. Sentence 1 is the most formal because it uses the word **elucidate**.

↓

1. **We do not know anything about** the mechanism.
2. **We do not know much about** the mechanism.
3. **There is not much data on** the mechanism.
4. **There is no data on** the mechanism.
5. **We are still working on** the mechanism.
6. **We are still studying** the mechanism.
7. **We are still analyzing** the mechanism.

'~에 대해서는 모른다'고 말할 때는 '우리는 ~에 대해서는 모른다'(1, 2), '~에 대한 데이터가 없다'(3, 4), '우리는 ~에 대해서 연구 중이다'(5~7) 가운데 어느 하나의 표현으로 말하면 된다.

Example 1 is active and starts with the expression **we do not know**. The expression **is not fully understood** has been changed to **we do not know anything about / much about**. Example 5 uses the two-word verb **working on**, which has the same meaning as **studying** or **analyzing**. The sentence, **We are still working on the mechanism** is another way of saying **The mechanism is not fully understood**. The word **elucidated is too formal for an oral presentation**. Its frequency is low and mostly restricted to academic papers.

Elucidate라는 동사는 학술 논문을 작성할 때 쓰는 딱딱한 표현이므로 구두 발표에서는 일반적으로 사용하지 않는다.

- This issue has been addressed by a lot of / by many / by a number of theoretical chemists.

↓

1. A lot of theoretical chemists **are looking at** this problem/issue.
2. A lot of theoretical chemists **are working on** this problem/issue.
3. A lot of theoretical chemists **are doing research on** this problem/issue.
4. A lot of theoretical chemists **are studying** this problem/issue.

'~에 대해서는 많은 연구가 이루어졌다'라는 표현은 '많은 연구자가 ~에 대해 연구하였다'라고 능동태의 말로 바꾸는 것이 좋다. 이때 '연구하다'를 나타내는 동사는 looking at ~, working on ~, doing research on ~, studying ~ 등을 사용한다.

This sentence has been changed from passive to active. In order to reduce formality, I have changed the formal verb **address** to **looking at**, **working on**, **doing research on**, **studying**.

Note The expression, ***we are studying on***, is incorrect. The preposition **on** can be used in the following patterns: **This is a study on reliability. We carried out a study on reliability.** In both of the examples, the word **study** is a noun and is followed by the preposition **on**. The word **study** has two patterns.
1. To study + topic (this is a verb) Example, **A lot of theoretical chemists are studying this problem.**
2. A study on + topic (this is a noun) Example, **We did a study on rates of biodegradability.**

Study 뒤에 전치사 on을 붙일지는 study를 동사로 사용하는지 명사로 사용하는지에 따라 다르다. Study를 동사로 사용한다면 타동사이므로 on은 붙이지 않고(We study + topic), 명사로 사용한다면 전치사 on을 붙여야 한다(a study on + topic).

- The apparatus is equipped with a temperature gauge.

↓

1. There is a temperature gauge.
2. The apparatus has a temperature gauge.
3. The apparatus consists of a temperature gauge, (a) microcomputer and (a) monitor.

'장치에는 온도계가 탑재되어 있다.'는 논문에서는 **be equipped with**의 수동태 문장으로 작성하지만, 구두발표에서는 **is** 또는 **has**를 사용한 능동태 문장으로 말한다. 또한, 장치의 구성을 말할 때는 **3**과 같이 **consists of** 뒤에 구성 요소를 간단히 열거해도 된다.

You can reduce the formality of this sentence by deleting **equipped with**. The sentence has been simplified by deleting the expression **equipped with** and using the verbs **is**, **has** and **consists of**. If the apparatus has a number of functions, you can use **consists of** and a simple list of components as in example 3.

- It is possible to purchase an SD card whose capacity is in excess of 40 GB.
- It is possible to purchase an SD card the capacity of which is in excess of 40 GB.

↓

1. You can buy an SD card that has over **40 GB**.
2. You can buy an SD card that has capacity over **40 GB**.
3. You can buy an SD card with capacity over **40 GB**.

It is possible → You can
purchase → buy
is in excess of → over

The phrases **whose capacity is in excess of** and **the capacity of which is in excess of** are usually used in written scientific English. They have been deleted and the new sentence pattern starts with the word **you**. The word **purchased** has been changed to **buy**. The expression **whose capacity is in excess of 40 GB** has been changed to **has over 40 GB**.

▪ We adopted a new system.

↓

1. **We used** a new system.
2. **We chose** a new system.
3. **We employed** a new system.

동사 adopt 대신에 use, choose, employ를 사용하고 있다. Use와 employ는 거의 같은 의미이지만 employ는 약간 딱딱한 표현이다.

The word **adopted** has been changed to, **used**, **chose**, **employed**. **Use** and **employ** have the same meaning, but **employ** is a lot more formal.

▪ Differences in performance were observed.
▪ Differences in performance were noted.
▪ Differences in performance were seen.

↓

1. **There were** differences in performance.
2. **There were** variations in performance.
3. **Performance varied.**
4. **We observed** differences in performance.
5. **We noted** differences in performance.
6. **We saw** differences in performance.

'~가 관찰되었다', '~가 보였다'는 수동태의 논문식 표현이므로, 구어체로는 '~가 있었다'(1, 2) 또는'우리는 ~을 관찰했다'(4~6)와 같이 말한다.

'~의 차이가 관찰되었다'를 '~가 변화했다'고 바꾸어 말하면, 3처럼 간결하게 표현할 수 있다.

In the first three examples, the verbs **observed**, **noted** and **seen** are not used.
Example 3 is the shortest and easiest to say. **Performance varied**.
In examples 4~6, the verbs **observed**, **noted** and **saw** are used in active sentences.

- Here we have the experimental setup. Its length is 14 meters.

1. **The experimental setup is 14 meters in length.**
2. **The setup is 14 meters in length.**
3. **The setup is 14 meters long.**
4. **The setup is 14 meters.**

원래 문장이 전반부는 구어체의 표현이지만 후반부가 논문식 표현이다. '길이는 ~m이다'라고 말할 때는 구어체로 왼쪽의 1~4와 같이 표현한다.

There is a big difference in the formality of the sentences **Here we have the experimental setup** and **Its length is 14 meters.** The first, **Here we have the experimental setup**, is informal and the second, **Its length is 14 meters**, is formal and mostly restricted to written scientific usage. The 4 example sentences are less formal. The most informal sentence is the last one. **The setup is 14 meters.**

- Another experiment was performed.
- Another experiment was carried out.

1. **We did another experiment.**

'실험을 했다'는 표현은 논문에서는 **performed** 또는 **carried out** 등의 수동태로 쓰지만, 구두발표에서는 단순하게 **We did ~**로 말하는 것이 좋다.

The verbs **performed** and **carried out** are formal and mostly used in written English.

The verb **did** is informal and easier to use. You can repeat the verb **do** several times. This is quite normal in an oral presentation. For example: **We did an experiment on X. We also did several experiments on Y. The next day, we did a follow-up experiment.** In this case, the word **did** is used three times. Repetition of verbs such as **do** and **look at** is not a problem in an oral presentation.

왼쪽의 예시에서는 동사 **do ~**를 3번이나 연속해서 사용하고 있지만, 구두발표에서는 **do ~** 또는 **look at ~**을 여러 번 반복 사용해도 괜찮다.

- Data was obtained from several different locations.

↓

1. We gathered data from several different locations.
2. We collected data from several different locations.
3. We took data from several different locations.
4. We got data from several different locations.

'자료를 수집했다'를 obtained보다 쉬운 동사인 gathered, collected, took, got 등으로 표현하고 있다 (got은 get의 과거형).

The verb **obtained** has been changed to **gathered**, **collected**, **took**, **got**. The example sentences are all active. The most informal verb is **got**. Please note that **got** is the past tense of **get**.

- It can be classified into 2 types.
- It can be divided into 2 types.

↓

1. There are 2 types.

'○개의 종류로 분류된다'(be classified into ~ types)는 '○개의 종류가 있다'(There are ~ types) 라고 바꾸어 말할 수 있다.

The verbs **classified into** and **divided into** have been deleted. The sentence has been reduced to four words. The simple pattern, **There is/are**, is a useful pattern for oral presentations.

이 예시처럼 구두발표에서 There is ~/are ~라고 하면 어떤 상태를 단적으로 표현할 때 매우 유용하다.

- This is an image of the electric power flow.

↓

1. Here you can see the electric power flow.
2. You can see the electric power flow here.
3. This is the electric power flow.
4. This shows the electric power flow.
5. Here we have the electric power flow.

The word image has been deleted in order to shorten the sentence and make it easier to say. The sentence has been reduced from nine words to six. **This is the electric power flow.**

슬라이드의 그림을 보여주며 '이것은 ~을 나타낸 그림입니다'(This is an image of ~)라고 말할 때 '~을 나타낸 그림'(an image of ~)을 생략하고 '이것은 ~입니다'(This is ~)라고 짧게 말해도 그 의미가 달라지지 않는다. 1~5에서는 an image of ~를 모두 생략하여 글자 수를 줄였다.

- It is said that the temperature will reach 30 degrees.
- It is thought that the temperature will reach 30 degrees.

↓

1. **People think that the temperature will probably reach 30 degrees.**
2. **We think the temperature will probably reach 30 degrees.**
3. **The temperature will probably reach 30 degrees.**

The expressions it is said and it is thought are too indirect. They are also unclear because it is not stated who the speaker is. These expressions are commonly found in academic papers and are too formal for oral presentations. Example 3 is the shortest. **The temperature will probably reach 30 degrees.**

'~라고 알려져 있다', '~라고 생각된다'(It is said ~/ It is thought ~) 등은 논문 작성에 많이 사용하는 표현이지만, 구두발표에서 사용하기에는 어감이 딱딱해서 적절치 않다. 또한, 이런 어투는 간접적인 표현이고 주체도 불명확하다. 따라서 구두발표에서는 주체가 분명한 능동태의 글로 바꾸거나(1, 2), 이 부분을 생략하고 단순하게 말한다(3).

▪ Machine accuracy is represented by this equation.

↓

1. This equation represents machine accuracy.
2. Here we have machine accuracy. (Use the pointer to highlight the equation)

원래 문장은 수동태이지만, 1처럼 어순을 바꾸어 능동태 문장으로 만든다.

슬라이드의 수식을 가장 간단하게 설명하려면, 2와 같이 레이저 포인터로 수식을 가리키면서 '이것은 ~입니다'(Here we have ~)라고 말하면 된다.

In this case, the presenter uses the pointer to indicate the equation and uses the simple sentence **Here we have** machine accuracy. The expression **Here we have is** extremely useful for describing what is on a powerpoint slide.

▪ We could demonstrate an increase in efficiency of over 12 percent.

↓

1. There was an increase in efficiency of over 12 percent.
2. There was a 12 percent increase in efficiency.
3. Efficiency increased by over 12 percent.

1~3에서는 '~를 나타낼 수 있었다'(We could demonstrate ~) 부분을 모두 생략하여 글자 수를 줄였다.

The expression **we could demonstrate** has been deleted. The word **could** is redundant. **Example 1** is much simpler and starts with **There was**. The shortest sentence is **Efficiency increased by over 12 percent**.

▪ More powerful batteries are required.

↓

1. We need more powerful batteries.

'~가 요구된다', '~가 필요하다' 등의 표현은 수동태의 are required ~라고 하지 말고, 능동태의 We need ~로 말한다.

The sentence has been changed from passive to active. The verb **required** has been changed to **need**.

- Stable cells are required for IPS regulation.
- IPS regulation requires stable cells.

1. For IPS regulation, you need stable cells.
2. You need stable cells for IPS regulation.
3. Stable cells are necessary for IPS regulation.

The sentence structure has been changed.The verb **required** has been changed to **need**.

이전의 예시와 마찬가지로 required 대신에 need 또는 necessary를 사용한다.

- A landslide occurred.

1. There was a landslide.

Example 1 starts with **there was**, and the word **occurred** has been deleted.

'산사태가 발생하였다'(A landslide occurred)를 '산사태가 있었다'(There was a landslide)로 바꿔서 occurred를 삭제하였다.

- With this system, it is possible to achieve a high degree of accuracy.

1. This system is highly accurate.
2. Using this system, you get a high degree of accuracy.
3. There is a high degree of accuracy with this system.

The phrase **It is possible to achieve** has been deleted. Example 1 is the shortest sentence and the easiest to say.

It is possible to achieve ~는 장황하고 딱딱한 표현이므로 1~3에서는 다른 표현으로 모두 바꿨다.

- The rocket receives 5 forces.

↓

1. There are 5 forces on the rocket.

The structure of the sentence has been simplified using the pattern **There are**. The word **receives** has been deleted.

문장의 구조를 바꾸어 There are ~로 시작하는 표현으로 만든다.

- A new approach was developed that achieved improved values.
- A new method was developed that realized improved values.

↓

1. Using this new method, we got improved values.
2. Using this new method, we obtained improved values.

The words **developed**, **achieved** and **realized** have been deleted. Example 1 is easier to say. The verbs **got** and **obtained** have been used in an active sentence using **we**. The word **got** is informal and frequently used.

수동태에서 능동태로 바꾸고, 동사도 achieved, realized 등에서 got, obtained 등으로 변경하였다. Got(get의 과거형)은 구어체의 표현이어서 구두발표에서 많이 사용한다.

- Biodegradable samples were successfully produced.

↓

1. We produced biodegradable samples.
2. We were able to produce biodegradable samples.

The sentence has been changed from passive to active using **we**. The word **successfully** has been deleted. In example 2, the phrase **we were able to produce** covers the meaning of the word **successfully**.

1, 2에서는 We로 시작하는 능동태 문장으로 모두 바꿨는데, successfully(성공적으로, 순조롭게)라는 느낌을 주고 싶을 때는 2처럼 We were able to produce ~라고 하면 된다.

Part 3

Simple ways to improve your slides
슬라이드 작성 요령

In this section, I introduce ways of improving your slides.

슬라이드를 만들 때 문법이나 영어 표현에 관련된 몇 가지 간단한 규칙을 활용하면 슬라이드의 완성도를 높일 수 있다. 이번 장에서는 슬라이드를 만들 때 주의해야 할 11가지 사항에 관해 소개한다.

1 Number your slides
슬라이드에 번호를 붙인다

Numbering your slides makes it is easier for the audience to ask questions. You can do it like this 1/12, or like this 1. The top right-hand side of the slide is a common position. The bottom right is also possible. Here are some examples of questions where a slide number is referred to in the Q and A session.

(청중의 질문) ○번째 슬라이드에서 질문이 있습니다.

Step 1 | Step 2

- I have a question about slide 7. What is the average increase in temperature?
- My question is about slide 7. What is the average increase in temperature?
- Could you show me slide 7, (please)? What is the meaning of the data in column 2?
- In slide 7, you showed us some data on reliability. Does that include all experiments?

In the above examples, **there are 2 steps**. In step 1, **the speaker refers to the slide number**. In step 2, **the speaker asks a short, direct question**. This 2-step system makes it easier for people to ask questions, and reduces the chances of miscommunication.

Note It is not correct to say *page* 7. The correct expression is slide 7.
Also please note that the pattern, Could you show me slide 7?, is more frequent than the pattern, Please show me slide 7. Both are grammatically correct. There is no difference in meaning.

슬라이드에 번호를 매겨 놓으면 청중이 그 번호를 지정하여 질문할 수 있어서 질의응답을 효율적으로 진행할 수 있다.

2 A space is needed between a number and a word
숫자 · 기호와 단어 사이에는 띄어쓰기를 한다

If you use a number and a word in the slide title, you should avoid the following mistake.

띄어쓰기 없음

× 2.Research goals

○ 2. Research goals

띄어쓰기 있음

There is no space between the period and the following word. This is a relatively minor error but it looks bad. Here is another example.

띄어쓰기 없음

× Travel record: time, position(longitude).

○ Travel record: time, position (longitude).

띄어쓰기 있음

You will note that there is no space between the word **position** and the **parenthesis**.

숫자와 단어 사이, 기호(마침표, 괄호 등)와 단어 사이는 반드시 띄어야 한다.

3 Use the slide title box to show the section
슬라이드의 가장 위 여백을 유용하게 활용하자

At the top of a slide, there is a box for the title. Recently, I noticed that presenters make use of the **top left part of the slide to indicate the part of the presentation** such as **Introduction**, **Results 1**, **Results 2**, **Discussion**. This will help your audience to follow the structure of the presentation. Here are some examples.

- **Introduction: Research background**
- **Results 1: Data on erosion / Erosion data**
- **Results 2: Data from field studies / Field study data**
- **Discussion: The issue of diffusion / Diffusion**

Using the title box to indicate the part of the presentation is a useful technique that helps the audience to follow.

슬라이드의 맨 위 여백에 Introduction, Methods, Results 등의 목차를 써넣으면 청중이 발표의 구성을 쉽게 파악할 수 있다.

4 Use of the definite article the in slide titles
슬라이드 제목에서 정관사 the의 사용법에 주의하자

I am often asked about the use of definite articles. It is difficult to give rules that work for every situation, but I would like to point out one issue that concerns the use of articles in slide titles.

Example slide titles

- The modified apparatus
- The advantages of the system
- The measurement procedure
- The open-case method

In the above examples, the sentences start with the definite article **the**. Titles in powerpoint presentations are generally **as short as possible**, and **definite articles are often omitted to reduce the length** of the sentence. So, **The modified apparatus** should be **Modified apparatus**. However, when you are introducing the slide, **you use** the definite article **the**. Let's look at an example of a **slide title and a script**.

Slide title **Modified apparatus**

Script So, let's move on to the next slide. **Here we have the modified apparatus**. As you can see, it consists of 6 items and the overall size has been reduced by about one third.

In the script, the definite article **the** is used before 'modified apparatus', but in the slide it is omitted.

슬라이드 제목은 가능하면 단순하게 표현하기 위해 정관사 the를 생략하는 경우가 많지만, 구두발표용 원고에는 the를 넣도록 한다.

5 Using contractions on slides: These samples aren't biodegradable

슬라이드에는 단축형 표현을 사용하지 말자

Contractions are sometimes called **short forms**. They are used in everyday conversation and informal writing such as text messages. They are generally not used in formal writing, such as academic papers, poster presentations, and powerpoint slides. Here are some examples.

단축형

✕ We couldn't get a clear image of the reaction.
○ We could not get a clear image of the reaction.

비단축형

✕ It's important to weigh the sample first.
○ It is important to weigh the sample first.

✕ This setup doesn't have a temperature gauge.
○ This setup does not have a temperature gauge.

This means that **you should not use a short form** in your powerpoint slides. However, it is common to use short forms when you are speaking.

It is ~ → It's ~ 등의 단축형은 구어체 표현이므로 학회의 발표 슬라이드 작성 시에는 사용할 수 없다. 다만 슬라이드를 말로 설명할 때는 사용해도 괜찮다.

6 Slide title: Singular or plural? 'S' or no 'S'?

슬라이드 제목은 단수형? 아니면 복수형?

Incorrect use of singular and plural nouns is common in slide titles. When introducing a topic **for the first time**, it is normal to use **plural** nouns because a general statement is being made. In the following 3 examples, the nouns **measurement**, **battery** and **neuron** should be plural. As this information is being introduced for the first time, **the plural noun is used as a general statement**. The singular noun is used in a case that is specific.

단수형

✕ The importance of reliable measurement

○ **The importance of reliable measurements**

복수형

✕ How to evaluate lithium battery

○ **How to evaluate lithium batteries**

✕ What is neuron?

○ **What are neurons?**

✕ Advantage of the revised system

○ **Advantages of the revised system**

명사는 단수형과 복수형을 주의해서 구분해야 한다. 그 단어가 가리키는 전체에 대해 일반적인 이야기를 할 때는 복수형을, 특정한 부분만을 이야기할 때는 단수형을 사용한다.

7 The word of can be a problem
전치사 of의 사용법에 주의하자

The word of is frequently misused in slide titles. Here are some examples.

이때 of는 잘못 사용함

× Concept *of* study

○ **Study concept/concepts**

어순을 바꾸어 of를 삭제

× Introduction *of* research

○ **Research introduction**

× Background *of* research

○ **Research background**

× Experiment *of* wave form

○ **Wave form experiments**

In the following 2 examples, the words introduction and approaches are followed by to and not of.

✕ Introduction *of* carbon nanotubes
○ Introduction to carbon nanotubes

Introduction 뒤에는 전치사 to를 붙여야 함

✕ Approaches *of* TAG production
○ Approaches to TAG production
○ TAG production

The correct preposition after the word **approaches** is **to**. It is possible to delete the word approaches and shorten the title to **TAG production.**

✕ Increase *of* self-sufficiency
○ Increase in self-sufficiency

Increase 뒤에는 전치사 in을 붙여야 함

✕ Increase *of* temperature
○ Increase in temperature
○ Temperature increase

The word increase takes the preposition in. For example, There was an increase in temperature of 2 degrees. There was an increase in yield of 20 percent.

전치사 of를 잘못 사용하는 경우가 많다. 어순을 바꾸어 of를 삭제하는 것이 좋은 경우, of가 아니라 다른 전치사를 사용해야 하는 경우(예: introduction to, approaches to, increase in) 등에 주의한다.

8 Avoid using the words my or our in slides

슬라이드에는 my 또는 our를 사용하지 말자

As a general rule, it is better not to use **my** or **our** in slide titles. Here are some examples.

슬라이드를 작성할 때는 my라는 용어를 사용하지 않음

✕ My experimental set up
○ Experimental setup

✕ Our current research status
○ Current research status

Note In the above examples, the words **my** and **our** are unnecessary. For more examples see page 16. Column: The word **my** is frequently misused.

일반적으로 슬라이드에서는 my 또는 our를 사용하지 않는다. 자세한 내용은 16쪽 칼럼을 참고한다.

9 Exclamation marks are not used in academic presentations or written papers

학회 발표에서는 느낌표 부호를 사용하지 않는다

Exclamation marks are used after a sentence, word or expression that expresses, **surprise**, **anger** or **excitement**, and are usually not used in academic English in either papers or presentations. However, I often see examples like these.

✕ Yield reached 10 per cent!!!
✕ We achieved an increase of 25 degrees!!!
✕ Thank you for your attention!!!!!!!

This use of exclamation marks creates an unprofessional, casual impression. In the examples given here, the exclamation marks have no meaning or function, and should be deleted.

느낌표(!) 부호는 격식이 없는 느낌을 주므로 학회 발표나 논문 같은 학술 분야에서는 사용하지 않는 것이 좋다.

10 Problems with question marks: Is this a statement or a question?

물음표 부호를 잘못 사용하지 않도록 주의하자

Many presenters use questions in their slides in order to get the attention of the audience. This is good because it focuses the audience's attention on a specific point. Here are some examples of mistakes where question marks are not needed.

How to ...는 의문형이 아니므로 '?'를 붙일 수 없음

✕ How to evaluate field measurements?

○ **How can we evaluate field measurements?**

이 문장은 의문형이므로 '?'가 있어야 함

✕ How to develop a more reliable system?

○ **How can we develop a more reliable system?**

In both of the above examples, the sentences **are not questions. They are statements.** The pattern **How to + verb** is not a question. To turn these sentences into questions, you need to add the question word **can**.

Here are some more examples.

✕ How to achieve higher efficiency?
○ **How can higher efficiency be achieved?**
○ **How can we get/obtain higher efficiency?**

✕ Where to position the detector?
○ **What is the best place to position the detector?**

✕ Why a catalyst is important?
○ **Why is a catalyst important?**

It is important to check if the sentence you put on a slide is a question or not. I frequently see presenters put a question mark after a sentence that is a statement and not a question.

물음표(?) 부호를 활용하면 청중의 관심은 끌 수 있지만, 의문형이 아닌 표현에 붙이지 않도록 주의한다.

11 Summary sentences at the bottom of slides: How to reduce the number of words

슬라이드 아래쪽에 요약을 넣자

It is common to put a summary sentence at the bottom of some slides. However, some presenters use full sentences with difficult vocabulary, which makes it hard for the audience to follow. These sentences sometimes take up a lot of space and make the slides look busy.

Here, I show how to reduce the length of summary sentences. First, **I show the original sentence**, then **the revised sentence** and **the script**.

Example 1

Original sentence ▶ 고치기 전의 요약문, 문장이 너무 길

We consider that reliability increases over a wide range.

Revised sentence ▶ 고친 후의 요약문, 글자 수가 줄어 간결함

Reliability increases over a wide range.

Script ▶ 위 요약문을 설명할 때 사용하는 원고의 예시

I'd like to stress that **reliability increases over a wide range.**

In example 1, the expression, **We consider that**, has been deleted from the original sentence. This reduces the length of the sentence.

Example 2

Original sentence

A new system of measurement was developed with improved accuracy of over 15 percent.

Revised sentence

New measurement system improved accuracy by over 15 percent.

Script

So, we developed a new measurement system that improved accuracy by over 15 percent.

In example 2, the original sentence pattern has been **changed from passive to active**. The word **developed** has been deleted.

Example 3

Original sentence

It is thought that the addition of an extra catalyst improves the reaction.

Revised sentence

Addition of an extra catalyst improves the reaction.

Script

We found that using an extra catalyst improves the reaction.

In example 3, the expression, **It is thought that**, has been deleted. This makes the sentence shorter.

Example 4

Original sentence

It is suggested that with early intensive rehabilitation patients can be discharged from hospital up to a week earlier.

Revised sentence

Patients having early intensive rehabilitation can leave hospital earlier.

Script

With early intensive rehabilitation patients can be discharged a week early.

The expression, It is suggested, has been deleted.

The easiest way to reduce the number of words in a summary slide is to delete expressions such as these: **we consider that**, **was developed**, **it is thought that**, **it is suggested that**.

슬라이드 아래쪽에 짧은 문장의 요약을 넣으면 청중이 내용을 이해하기 쉽다. 어려운 단어를 피하고, 단어 수를 줄이는 것이 좋다.

Column #03

A Summary-box and mini-summary can help the audience follow your presentation

Summary-box와 mini-summary를 활용하자

It's late October, and I am seeing over 10 presentations a week. Last week's standout presentation was by an associate professor at a national university on the subject of cancer cells. I found the content matter to be quite challenging, but the presenter did two things that really helped me to follow. The first one was to provide summaries at the bottom of some but not all slides. Summary boxes are especially useful at the end of a sequence of slides.

Here is an example.

Summary-box의 예

Single infection of vectors make it possible to induce safe differentiated cells efficiently

The use of summary boxes helped me to understand the presentation.

Another technique that I found really useful was the presenter's use of mini-summaries. Typically, the presenter provided short mini-summaries of important information at the end of a section including several slides. Here are some example sentences used by the presenter to signal the start of a mini-summary.

Mini-summary를 말할 때의 예

- Taken together this data shows the following: + (list of main points)
- I'll summarize the significance of these results. + (list of main points)
- In total this means that...
- Taken as a whole this means that...
- Totally, this information suggests that...

발표 과정에서 앞서 설명한 내용을 적절히 요약하면 청중이 이해하기 쉽다. 다음 두 가지 기술을 활용할 수 있다.

Summary-box: 슬라이드 아래쪽에 텍스트 상자를 만들어 간단한 요약문을 넣는다. 모든 슬라이드에 넣을 필요는 없고, 각 주제가 끝날 때 삽입하는 것이 좋다.
Mini-summary: 말로 요약을 한다. 이것도 하나의 주제가 끝나는 시점에 끼워 넣어야 효과가 좋다.

Part 4

How to improve the clarity of the main body

본론을 알기 쉽게 전달하는 방법

The main body is the longest part of an oral presentation. It contains a lot of information and, unless it is carefully structured, can be difficult for the audience to follow. The examples in this section will **improve the clarity of the main body**.

발표의 본론(main body)에는 많은 정보가 포함되어 있으므로 이를 정확하게 요약하여 청중이 알기 쉽게 전달해야 한다. 이 장에서는 논리적으로 내용을 전개하는 표현, 슬라이드의 정보를 설명하는 표현 등 본론을 설명하는 데 필요한 여러 표현과 예문을 소개한다.

1 Starting a new topic, section
새로운 주제/항목을 시작하는 방법

The sentences introduced in this section are important because they help the audience to understand the structure of the presentation.

여기에서는 청중이 발표의 구성을 쉽게 파악할 수 있도록 주제 전환에 사용하는 표현을 소개한다.

1.1 How to introduce a new section / topic
새로운 주제/항목으로 넘어간다

이어서 ~에 대해 말씀드리겠습니다.

So that's all I have to say about the methods we used.

- **Next, I'm going to move on to** the results and discussion.

Examples

- **Now, I'm going to go on to** the results and discussion.
- **Next, I'm going to look at** the results and discussion.
- **Next, I want to look at** the results and discussion.
- **Let's look at** the results and discussion.
- **Let's take a look at** the results and discussion.

다음의 주제/항목으로 넘어갈 때는 (구동사) + (주제/항목) 형태로 말하는 것이 좋다. 구동사는 일반적으로 move on to ~, go on to ~, look at ~, take a look at ~ 등을 활용한다. 주제/항목의 부분은 the next section(다음 항목), Part 3, the results and discussion 등과 같이 구체적인 번호/내용으로 표현한다.

The most common verbs to indicate you are moving on to a new topic or section are as follows: **move on to**, **go on to**, **look at**, **take a look at**. They are usually followed by these expressions: **the next section**, **part 3**, **the results and discussion**, **applications**, **results from experiment 1**.

1.2 How to move on to the next slide
다음 슬라이드로 넘어간다

Here, I show how to make a transition to the next slide.

~에 대해서는 다음 슬라이드에서 말씀드리겠습니다.

One of our main objectives was to reduce the thickness of the substrate. This required various approaches.

- We/you can see that information in the next slide.
- I'll show you that information in the next slide.

Examples

- I'll show you some more data on that in the next slide.
- I'll show you more data on reliability in the next slide.
- I'll show you some more reliability data in the next slide.
- I'll show you the approaches we used in the next slide.
- I'll focus on that data in the next slide.
- I'll introduce that data in the next slide.
- I'll describe the reaction in the next slide.

'○○에 대해서는 다음 슬라이드에서 말씀드리겠습니다'라는 표현은 We (You) can see ~/ I'll show you (+ topic) in the next slide라고 말한다.

Note The preposition on is used in the following way.

- I'll show you more data on reliability.
- I'll give you some more information on rates of recurrence.

'~에 내한 정보/데이터'라고 발할 때는 전치사 on을 사용하여 왼쪽처럼 표현한다.

Common errors — 흔히 하는 실수

✕ ***From now on,*** I am going to move on to the results and discussion.

✕ ***From now,*** I am going to move on to the results and discussion.

○ **Next,** I am going to move on to the results and discussion.

○ **Now,** I am going to move on to the results and discussion.

✕ I'm going to ***move to*** the results and discussion.

○ I'm going to **move on to** the results and discussion.

✕ I'm going to ***go to*** the results and discussion

○ I'm going to **go on to** the results and discussion.

The expressions ***From now on*** / ***From now*** are unnatural in the context of a presentation. It is more natural to use **next** / **now** / **I'm going to move on to**. Please note that ***move to*** should be **move on to** and that ***go to*** should be **go on to**. Both **move on to** and **go on to** are 3-word verbs and the words **on** and **to** should not be omitted.

'지금부터'라는 표현을 *From now on* 또는 *From now*라고 말하면 학회 발표에서는 자연스럽지 않다. Next 또는 Now로 표현하는 것이 좋다.

Move to ~ 또는 *go to* ~는 어떤 물체가 위치를 이동할 때 사용하는 표현이다. 따라서 '다음 주제로 넘어가겠다'라고 할 때는 move on to ~ 또는 go on to ~로 표현하므로 on을 빠뜨리지 않도록 주의한다.

1.3 How to introduce a topic that covers several slides: using the expression in the next few slides
여러 장의 슬라이드로 길게 언급하는 내용으로 넘어간다

In the above section, I focused on introducing single slides. In some cases, it will take several slides to cover a single topic. You can use the expression, in the next few slides, to introduce a topic that covers several slides. This expression **tells the audience that you will introduce several slides that cover the same information/topic.** In the next few slides can be used at the start or end of a sentence. A similar expression is over the next few slides. You can be more specific with the expressions: over the next three slides and in the next three slides. Here is an example.

하나의 내용(예: 실험 A의 결과)을 여러 장의 슬라이드로 이어서 설명할 수 있다. 이 경우, 아래의 예문처럼 청중에게 말하면 된다.

'다음 몇 장의 슬라이드'는 in the next few slides 또는 over the next few slides로 표현한다. In the next three slides와 같이 few 대신에 구체적인 숫자(슬라이드 장수)를 넣어도 된다. 어느 경우든 복수형 slides로 써야 하니 주의한다.

다음 몇 장의 슬라이드에서는 ~에 대해 말씀드리겠습니다.

That covers the main issues of cost and manufacturing.

- In the next few slides, I want to focus on reliability.

Examples

- In the next few slides, I'll show you some data on reliability.
- In the next few slides, I'll focus on reliability.
- In the next three slides, I'll talk about / discuss the issue of reliability.
- I'll show you some data on reliability in the next few slides.
- Over the next few slides, I'll focus on reliability.
- In the next few slides, I'll discuss modifications to the system.

2 Explaining what is on a slide
슬라이드의 정보를 설명하는 방법

Here I introduce useful expressions for explaining what is on a slide.

2.1 Use the expression Here we have to introduce the main information on a slide
슬라이드의 정보를 설명한다

One of the easiest and quickest ways to introduce the main information on a slide is with the expression **Here we have + (information)**. This is an example.

> 슬라이드에서 설명하려는 부분을 레이저 포인터로 가리키면서 **Here we have + (information)**라고 표현하는 것이 정보를 설명하는 가장 간단한 방법이다.

Script(슬라이드의 데이터를 레이저 포인터로 가리키면서 설명하는 예시)

This slide shows data taken from our field experiments. Here we have temperature, (here) precipitation and (here) windspeed.

In this example, **here** can be said once only, or repeated three times. Both are possible. In the example below, the word **here** is said only once and not repeated. This makes the sentence shorter. It is important to use the pointer as you speak to indicate temperature, precipitation and windspeed on the slide.

> **Here we have** ~라는 표현으로 여러 부분을 연속해서 설명할 때는 두 번째 이후로는 **here**를 생략할 수 있다.

Script(위 원고에서 두 번째 이후에 here를 생략한 경우)

This slide shows data taken from our field experiments. Here we have temperature, precipitation, and windspeed.

The biggest advantage of the expression **Here we have** is that it avoids the use of difficult expressions such as these:

the bottom right panel shows and **the upper left image depicts**.

The bottom right panel shows the annual rainfall, can be changed to, **Here we have annual rainfall**.

Here are 4 examples of formal expressions that can be changed to informal English using the expression, **Here we have**.

한 장의 슬라이드에서 여러 정보를 설명할 때는 **the upper left image**(왼쪽 위의 그림) 등으로 슬라이드의 특정 부분을 이야기하는지 꼭 집어서 말해야 한다. 따라서 레이저 포인터로 해당 부분을 가리키면서 **Here we have ~**의 표현으로 설명하면 이런 수고를 줄일 수 있다.

The upper left image depicts the annual rainfall.	→	**Here we have annual rainfall.**
The upper line shows the annual rainfall.	→	**Here we have annual rainfall.**
The lower line shows the annual rainfall.	→	**Here we have annual rainfall.**

The underlined expressions on the left are too formal, and quite difficult to say. You can avoid them by using the phrase – **Here we have annual rainfall**. Please remember to **use the pointer** to show which part of the slide you are referring to.

(레이저 포인터로 가리키며) 이것은 ~을 나타내고 있습니다.

- **Here we have** temperature **and (here)** precipitation.
- **Here we have** the main results.
- **Here are** the main results.
- **Here we have** the experimental setup.
- **Here is** the experimental setup.

첫 번째 예문은 한 문장으로 두 부분을 설명하므로 두 번째 **here**는 생략할 수 있다.

Here we have ~ 대신에 **Here are/is ~**라고도 표현할 수 있다.

Note Both patterns can be used:

- Here we have the main results.
- Here are the main results.

A similar sentence to **Here we have** is **This slide shows + (topic)**. Some presenters overuse the expression **This slide shows**. You should try to get a balance by using **Here we have** as well as **This slide shows**. Please note that **This slide shows** is usually **used once only in each slide to introduce the main topic**, which is probably written in the slide box at the top of the slide. It is not appropriate to use it several times in one slide. The expression **Here we have** can be used **several times in the same slide** to move on to different information. In the example below, **here we have** is used 3 times to focus on different parts of the same slide.

Here we have ~와 비슷한 표현으로 This slide shows ~가 있는데, 이 표현은 사용법이 서로 다르니 주의해야 한다. This slide shows ~라는 말은 그 슬라이드 자체의 내용(예: '실험 방법')을 설명할 때 쓰는 표현이므로 보통 한 장의 슬라이드에 한 번만 사용해야 한다. 이에 비해, here we have ~는 한 장의 슬라이드에서 여러 도표나 그림 등을 설명할 때 쓰는 말이므로 한 장의 슬라이드에서도 여러 번 반복해서 사용할 수 있다.

Script(같은 슬라이드에서 여러 번 here we have ~를 사용하는 예시)

Here we have data from the first experiment. And here, (we have) data from the second experiment, which was done ten days later. And over here, we have average values.

Please note that there are 2 ways of saying the second sentence. You can reduce the length of the sentence by saying, **And here, data from the second experiment**. Or you can say the sentence in full like this. **And here, we have data** from the second experiment.

Here we have ~라는 표현으로 두 개의 문장을 이어서 설명하는 경우에 And here, we have ~로 하되, we have ~는 생략하고 간단하게 And here, ~라고 말할 수도 있다.

Common errors — 흔히 하는 실수

X Here *shows* temperature.
O **Here we have temperature.**
O **This slide shows temperature.**

The word **here** should be followed by **we have**. It is not possible to say ***Here shows***.
In the expression **here we have**, the word **we** includes both the presenter and the audience. The expression **Here you have** is possible, but less frequent.

Here shows ~라고 하면 잘못된 표현이다. Here 뒤에는 we have를 이어서 말해야 한다(Here you have ~라고 할 수도 있지만 이런 표현은 별로 사용하지 않는다). 동사 show는 This slide shows ~등의 표현으로 사용한다.

2.2 How to move on to other information in the same slide using short questions such as: How about X? What about X?
같은 슬라이드에서 다른 항목의 내용으로 옮기는 표현

Since slides have a lot of information, you need to move logically and clearly through the material shown. Using simple expressions such as **How about X?** and **What about X?** will signal to the audience that you are moving on to another part of the slide. They are particularly useful if you have a lot of information in columns, lists or tables.

같은 슬라이드 안에서 다른 항목으로 내용을 옮길 때는 **How about X?** 또는 **What about X?**와 같이 의문형으로 말한다.

Example 1 (다른 내용으로 옮기기 위해 의문문을 활용하는 예시 1)

In this slide, we have results from four different locations A to D at different times of year. Locations A and B have standard values. How about locations C and D? As you can see, the values for C and D are quite different. For example, windspeed and temperature were significantly higher.

Example 2 (다른 내용으로 옮기기 위해 의문문을 활용하는 예시 2)

Here we have the main data from groups A and B. The values are what we would expect. In other words, there are no significant changes. How about group C? Well, at this point, we start to see some significant differences. I'll look at those differences in the next slide.

Using the expressions **How about X?** and **What about X?** helps to avoid a flat, monotonous presentation. There is no difference in meaning between the questions **How about X?** and **What about X?**

의문형을 활용하면 발표가 단조로워지는 것을 피할 수 있다.

2.3 How to introduce another topic in the slide using as for, in terms of, in the case of, as far as, from the viewpoint of
슬라이드의 다른 내용을 언급한다

In this section, the expressions can be used to introduce other information or topics on the same slide.

Script(As for ~를 이용하여 새로운 내용을 언급하는 예시)

We have seen that the apparatus is more reliable, and also robust, particularly at low temperatures. As for energy consumption, it is marginally more efficient.

In the above example, a new topic **energy consumption** is introduced with the expression **as for**. Other expressions are listed below.

한편, ○○(지금까지 설명했던 내용과 다른 주제)에 대해 말하자면 ~입니다.

- As for energy consumption, it is marginally more efficient.
- In terms of energy consumption, it is marginally more efficient.
- As far as energy consumption is concerned, it is marginally more efficient.
- From the viewpoint of energy consumption, it is marginally more efficient.
- From the energy consumption point of view, it is marginally more efficient.
- Regarding energy consumption, it is marginally more efficient.
- Concerning energy consumption, it is marginally more efficient.
- In the case of energy consumption, it is marginally more efficient.

'한편, ~에 대해 말하자면'이라고 하면서 새로운 내용으로 넘어갈 때는 왼쪽의 여러 표현을 활용할 수 있다. As for ~ 또는 In terms of ~가 가장 간단하면서도 많이 사용하는 표현이다.

Of these expressions, as for and in terms of are shorter, easier to say, and more frequently used.

Note The expression in the case of requires the word the. The expression in case of is used like this. In case of fire, leave the building immediately. You cannot say *In case of* energy consumption. The correct expression is as follows: In the case of energy consumption. Correct use of the definite article the is important when using the expression in the case of.

In the case of ~와 비슷한 표현으로 in case of ~가 있는데, in case of ~는 in case of fire(화재의 경우)처럼 '만일 ~가 일어났을 경우에'라는 가정법의 느낌을 준다. 따라서 단순히 '~의 경우는'이라고 말할 때는 in the case of ~를 사용한다.

2.4 Explain what is on the slide: Using the expressions X is in blue and X is shown in blue

글자/선의 색깔에 관해 설명한다.

Information shown on a slide is often represented by a color, type of font, or type of line such as a dotted line. Here I focus on easy ways to introduce what is on a slide when it is represented by a color, type of font or type of line.

구두발표의 슬라이드에서는 글자 색깔의 차이에 어떤 의미가 있을 수 있다(예: 수치가 증가한 곳을 파란색 글자로 표시한다). 따라서 글자 색깔의 차이를 설명할 때는 왼쪽과 같은 표현을 활용한다.

변경된 부분은 파란색 글자로 표시하였습니다.

This is the previous experimental setup. On the right we have the updated setup.

- Modifications to the system are in blue.
- Modifications to the system are shown in blue.

글자 또는 선의 색깔에 관해 설명할 때는 are in (+ 색깔 이름) 또는 are shown in (+ 색깔 이름)이라고 말한다.

As you can see from the example, the expressions are in + color and are shown in + color are used. The meaning is the same.

Here are some examples that use more formal verbs: show, indicate, depict, represent. These examples are grammatically correct, but are more appropriate for a written paper than an oral presentation.

- The blue line shows modification to the system.
- The blue line indicates modifications to the system.
- The blue line depicts modifications to the system.
- The blue line represents modifications to the system.

왼쪽과 같이 show, indicate, depict, represent 등의 용어도 '파란 선은 ~를 나타냅니다'라는 뜻으로 사용할 수 있으나 다소 딱딱한 표현이어서 구두발표에서는 적합하지 않다.

Each of the above 4 sentences can be changed to less formal patterns like these. **Modifications to the system are (shown) in blue.**

2.5 Explain what is on the slide: using in italics, in bold, in large font, underlined, by a dotted line

글꼴/선의 종류에 관해 설명한다.

Here are some examples using the expressions in italics, in bold, in large font, underlined and by a dotted line. These are useful expressions for focusing on particular information on a slide. The grammar pattern is the same as **are in blue** or **are shown in blue**.

~은 ○○(글꼴/선의 종류)로 표시하였습니다.

- Values are in italics / are shown in italics.
- Values are in bold / are shown in bold.
- Values are in large font / are shown in large font.
- Values are underlined.

글꼴(font: 볼드체, 이탤릭체 등)의 의미를 설명할 때도 글자 색깔과 마찬가지로 are in (+ 폰트의 종류) 또는 are shown in (+ 폰트의 종류)라고 말하면 된다.

> **Note** In this example, the word underline is a verb. The following expressions are incorrect:
>
> ✕ *Values are shown in underlined.*
> ✕ *Values are in underlined.*

밑줄의 의미를 설명할 때는 동사 underline을 이용해 are underlined ~로 표현한다. 밑줄의 경우에는 색깔 이름 / 글꼴 이름과는 다르게 are (shown) in (+ 명사)의 방식으로는 표현할 수 없으니 주의해야 한다.

- Values are shown by a dotted line.
- Values are represented by a dotted line.
- The dotted line shows values.
- The dotted line represents values.

선의 종류(점선 등)를 설명하는 경우는 are shown / represented by (+ 선의 종류) 또는 (선의 종류) + shows/represents로 표현한다.

Note The sentence, Values are represented by a dotted line, is quite long and not easy to say. You can avoid this and other sentences introduced in this section with the expression, **Here we have** values. Please remember to use the pointer as you say Here we have values.

또는 레이저 포인터로 선을 가리키면서 Here we have ~(이것은 ~입니다)라고 설명하면 간단하다.

2.6 How to refer to circles, triangles, squares, dots and arrows
도표 또는 그림 속의 기호를 설명한다

In graphs and figures, **circles, triangles, squares, dots** and **arrows** are used to indicate information. Here are some example sentences.

○○(기호의 종류)는 ~를 나타내고 있습니다.

- The red circles show temperature.
- The triangles indicate rate of increase.
- The squares show rate of increase.
- The dots indicate rate of increase.
- The arrows show areas of friction.

도표 또는 그림 속의 기호(원형, 삼각형, 화살표 등)가 무엇을 나타내는지 설명하려면 왼쪽과 같이 (기호 이름) + show/indicate ~라고 말한다.

In the above examples, **circles, triangles, squares, dots, and arrows are plural.** When explaining a graph or figure, in most cases you will use the plural form of **nouns** such as **circles, triangles, squares, dots** and **arrows.** This is because figures will normally have more than one circle, triangle, dot, square or arrow. The same is true for figure legends in papers. Of course, if there is only one circle, the correct exam-

보통은 하나의 도표/그림 속에 여러 개의 기호가 있을 수 있으므로 기호의 명칭은 복수형으로 표시한다(예: circles, arrows). 물론, 기호가 하나만 있으면 단수형으로 표현한다.

ple is as follows: **The red circle shows temperature**. But the frequency of this example is very low, since the majority of figures will have more than one circle.

Common errors — 흔히 하는 실수

✕ The ***circle*** shows temperature at various time points.
○ The **circles** show temperature at various time points.

In most figures, you will have **several circles, dots or triangles**. You cannot say, **the circle shows** if there is more than one circle in the figure.

✕ Values are ***written*** in red.
○ Values **are in red**.
○ Values **are shown in red**.

I frequently hear presenters say, ***Values are written in red***. This is incorrect. It should be, **Values are in red** or **Values are shown in red**.

그림 속에 여러 개의 동그라미가 있는 경우에 왼쪽의 The *circle* shows ~처럼 단수형을 표현하면 안 된다.

슬라이드의 문자 색깔을 설명할 때 *are written in* ~이라고 하면 안 되고, are in ~ 또는 are shown in ~으로 표현해야 한다.

3 How to use the word mean
동사 mean의 올바른 사용법

3.1 Mean: Common errors 1
Mean을 잘못 사용한 예시(1): 슬라이드에서 어떤 대상을 설명하는 경우

I'll start this section by focusing on common errors. The first involves using **means** to describe what is on a slide.

✕ The X axis ***means*** temperature.
○ The X axis **shows** temperature.
○ **Here we have** temperature.

✕ The dotted line ***means*** values.
○ The dotted line **represents** values.
○ Values **are represented by** a dotted line.
○ **Here we have** values.

✕ This graph ***means*** the dry weight of the sample.
○ This graph **shows** the dry weight of the sample.
○ **Here we have** the dry weight of the sample.

✕ The black circles ***mean*** rates of biodegradability in the samples.
○ The black cirlces **show / indicate / represent / denote** rates of biodegradability in the samples.

The above examples show that **mean** cannot be used to describe something physical on a slide such as **the X axis**, **values**, **dry weight of the sample** or **rates of biodegradability**. In that case, you need to use the words **show**, **indicate**, **depict** and **represent**. It is also easier and quicker to use the expression **here we have** + **temperature**, **val-**

슬라이드의 정보를 설명할 때 동사 **mean**(의미하다)을 잘못 사용하는 경우가 많다.

동사 **mean**은 정보와 데이터의 의미를 설명하는 데 사용한다. 즉, '이 실험 결과는 ~이라는 것을 의미합니다'와 같은 문장에서 mean을 사용하는 것은 적절하다. 왼쪽의 예처럼 'X축은 ~를 나타내고 있습니다', '점선은 ~를 나타내고 있습니다' 등의 경우에 슬라이드의 어떤 대상(object)이 무엇을 나타내고 있는지 설명할 때는 ***mean*** 대신에 **show**, **indicate**, **depict**, **represent**, **denote** 등의 동사를 활용해야 한다.

슬라이드에서 어떤 대상을 설명하는 경우는 이를 레이저 포인터로 가리키면서 **Here we have** ~라고 말하는 것이 가장 간단한 표현 방법이다(106~108쪽 참고).

ues, the dry weight of the sample, rates of biodegradability.

3.2 Mean: Common errors 2
Mean을 잘못 사용한 예시(2): 약어의 설명

Another common error with the word **mean** is as follows. In this case, people use the word **mean** to explain an acronym.

Acronym(두문자어)은 여러 문자의 앞글자만 따서 연결한 약자이다. 'AIST란 ~라는 뜻입니다/~의 약자입니다'처럼 두문자어의 정식 명칭을 설명할 때는 *mean*이 아니라 stand for ~ 또는 is short for ~를 사용한다(180쪽 참고).

- ✕ AIST ***means*** Advanced Institute of Science and Technology.
- ○ AIST **stands for** Advanced Institute of Science and Technology.
- ○ AIST **is short for** Advanced Institute of Science and Technology.

In this case, means cannot be used to introduce acronyms. The best way to introduce an acronym is with **stand for** or **is short for**.

3.3 Using mean to signal the start of an explanation
Mean의 올바른 사용법(1): 설명의 도입 부분에서 의문문으로 사용한다

Please note that **mean can be used in a question to signal the start of an explanation.** In the examples below, the presenter indicates that what follows is an explanation of data or information already presented.

이 결과는 무엇을 의미할까요?

- **What do the results mean?**
- **What do these figures mean?**
- **What does the sudden increase in temperature mean?**

구두발표에서는 결과를 설명할 때 왼쪽의 설명처럼 What do ~ mean?이라는 의문형 문장을 사용하면 청중의 관심을 이끌어낼 수 있다.

3.4 Using mean to explain some information or data
Mean의 올바른 사용법(2): 정보나 데이터를 설명한다

Mean is usually used to explain some information or data. Here are some examples in context.

Script(제시한 정보가 무엇을 의미하는지 설명하는 예시 1)

The brown staining shows that the sample has started to degrade. You can see the evidence of extensive brown staining on both sides of the sample. This means that the decomposition process has started.

In this case, the expression **this means that** is used to explain the information/data that has just been presented. So the presenter switches from **describing information** to **explaining that information** using the expression **This means that**.

Here is another example.

Script(제시한 정보가 무엇을 의미하는지 설명하는 예시 2)

If you look at the surface of the metal you can see some faint lines. Observation with a microscope shows that the lines penetrate toward the center of the sample. This means that the metal is fractured, and the risk of metal fatigue is extremely high.

In this example, the sentence, **Observation with a microscope shows that the lines penetrate toward the center of the sample**, is explained with the expression, **This means that the metal is fractured, and the risk of metal fatigue is extremely high**.

위의 두 예시처럼, **mean**은 정보나 데이터가 무엇을 의미하는지 설명할 때 사용한다. 위의 예시는 모두 '정보의 제시'(예: ~라는 관찰 결과를 얻었다) → '정보의 설명'(예: 이 결과는 ~이라는 것을 의미한다)의 순서로 되어 있으며, **mean**은 뒤의 문장에서 사용한다.

4 Useful expressions for explaining technical terms: by X, I mean, what do I mean by X?, in other words, X is defined as, I'm going to refer to X as Y 전문 용어를 설명하는 방법

4.1 Useful expressions for explaining technical terms 전문 용어를 설명할 때 편리한 표현

● By X, I mean X의 의미는 ~입니다.

It is important to explain any technical terms that the audience might not be familiar with. In the example below, a technical term, **relapse**, is introduced with the phrase, **By relapse, I mean** + explanation.

By (+ 전문 용어), I mean (+ 설명)의 형태로 용어의 정의/의미를 설명한다.

Script(By X, I mean의 표현으로 relapse라는 용어를 설명하는 예시)

We used different whitening treatments on 3 groups of patients. In groups 1 and 2, teeth remained white after treatment. In group 3, several of the patients suffered relapse. By relapse, I mean the process where the teeth returned to their original color after treatment.

The expression **by X, I mean** can be used in a question form like this. **What do I mean by X?** An example of that pattern is shown below.

● What do I mean by X? X는 무슨 뜻일까요?

Script(What do I mean by X?의 표현으로 relapse라는 용어의 설명을 시작하는 예시)

What do I mean by relapse? Well, the term relapse refers to a change in the color of the teeth after treatment.

The presenter introduces a technical term with a question **What do I mean by (technical term)?** and then provides a simple explanation of that term.

의문형으로 질문한 후에 설명을 시작하면 청중의 관심을 모을 수 있다.

● In other words 다시 말하면/즉

A less formal way of introducing a technical term is with the expression **in other words**.

In other words(다시 말하면/즉)를 사용하여 용어를 설명한다.

Script(in other word의 표현으로 relapse라는 용어를 설명하는 예시)

Relapse, in other words, the process where the teeth go back to the original color before treatment, is a serious issue.

In this example, the presenter explains a technical term starting with the expression **in other words**.

● X is defined as + (short definition) X는 ~로 정의한다

Script(X is defined as ~의 표현으로 X를 설명하는 예시)

Relapse is defined as the process where after treatment, the tooth partially returns to its original color.

The expression, (relapse) **is defined as**, is a formal way of explaining something.

(전문 용어) is defined as (+ 설명)는 용어의 정의를 설명하는 표현이다.

● I'm going to refer to X as Y X를 Y라고 부르기로 한다

Script(I'm going to refer to X as Y 형태로 degradation이라는 용어를 설명하는 예시)

You can see from the photos of the samples that there are some changes in color and also that the rough surface areas increased. I'm going to refer to this process as degradation.

In some cases, it is necessary to specify how you will refer to something, such as a process or phenomena.

오늘 발표에서는 X를 Y라고 부르기로 하겠습니다.

- I'm going to refer to this process as degradation.
- In this presentation, I'll use the word degradation to refer to changes in color and surface roughness of the samples.
- I'm going to use the term degradation to refer to changes in color and surface roughness of the samples.

Refer to X as Y로 'X(과정/현상의 설명)를 Y(전문 용어)라고 부른다'라는 의미가 된다.

왼쪽의 두 번째와 세 번째 예문처럼 use the word/term Y to refer to X의 형태로 사용하기도 한다. 이 경우 Y(전문 용어)가 앞에 온다.

Common errors ─ 흔히 하는 실수

✕ *Hereafter*, color change is referred to as degradation.

○ In this presentation, I will refer to color change as degradation.

○ In this presentation, color change is referred to as degradation.

○ From here on / From now on, color change is referred to as degradation.

The word hereafter is very formal and usually used in contracts or legal documents. It means from here on, from now on. It is too formal to use in an oral presentation. More appropriate expressions are as follows: in this presentation, from here on, from now on. The shortest way of specifying the use of a term or expression is like this. I will refer to (color change) as (degradation).

논문을 작성할 때 '이하, ~라고 부른다'라는 표현으로 hereafter를 사용하는데, 이는 딱딱한 표현이어서 구두발표에서는 적합하지 않다. 구두발표에서 '여기서부터는 / 이 발표에서는 ~라고 부릅니다'라고 말할 때는 '여기서부터는 / 이 발표에서는'이라는 표현은 in this presenation, from here on, from now on으로 말하고, '~라고 부릅니다'라는 표현은 I will refer to (+ 설명) as (+ 용어)로 말한다.

4.2 Defining a term using called, known as, referred to as, defined as

'X는 Y라고 부릅니다'의 형태로 정의를 설명하는 방법

There are several expressions for defining a term. Here I introduce four of the most frequent: **called**, **known as**, **referred to as**, **defined as**.

Script(called를 사용하여 relapse라는 용어를 설명하는 예시)

After bleaching, teeth may become several shades lighter. However, it is possible that teeth will partly return to their original color. This process is called relapse.

이 과정은 ~라고 부릅니다.

- This process is called relapse.
- This process is known as relapse.
- This process is referred to as relapse.
- This process is defined as relapse.

X is called Y, X is known as Y, X is referred to as Y, X is defined as Y 등은 'X는 Y라고 부른다'는 표현으로 전문 용어를 설명할 때 사용한다.

In the example, This process is called relapse, the word as is not used after called.

Common errors – 흔히 하는 실수

✕ This process is called *as* degradation.
○ This process **is called** degradation.
○ This process **is known as** degradation.
○ This process **is referred to as** degradation.
○ This process **is defined as** degradation.

위의 표현 중에 X is called Y의 경우에만 as가 없으니 주의한다.

The word **called** cannot be followed by **as**. The word **as** is used like this in the following expressions: is known as, is referred to as, is defined as, but after the word **call**, **as** is not necessary.

4.3 How to use the word define
동사 define의 사용법

The word define occurs frequently in scientific oral presentations. Here are some examples.

저희는 ~을 ~라고 정의했습니다.

- We define relapse as the degree to which a tooth has reverted to its original color after treatment.
- We define expert assessors as people with over 25 years' experience of evaluation.
- For the purposes of this experiment, we define people with over 25 years' experience of evaluation as expert.
- Expert assessors are defined as people with over 25 years' experience of evaluation.

동사 define(정의하다)은 전문 용어의 정의를 설명할 때 자주 사용한다.

동사 define을 수동태로 사용하면 X is defined as Y가 되고, 능동태로 사용하면 we define X as Y가 된다. 구두발표에서는 능동태 쪽이 적합하다.

Note In the passive, the pattern is as follows: X is defined as Y. For example, Color change and surface roughness are defined as degradation. In an active sentence, the structure is, we define X as Y. The active sentence, We define X as Y is better for oral presentations. For example, We define color change and surface roughness as degradation.

5 Simplifying and rephrasing the information you present
정보를 단순화하여 전달하는 방법 / 쉬운 표현으로 바꾸어 말하는 방법

An oral presentation is not the same as an academic paper. Readers of an academic paper are in control of the information in front of them, and can reread sections of the paper to check information. The audience at an oral presentation has no control over the information being presented. For this reason, **simplification of the information presented is necessary to help the audience follow**. In this section, I introduce examples of **how to simplify information**.

논문에서는 독자들이 문장을 반복해서 정독할 수 있지만, 구두발표에서는 그렇게 할 수 없으므로 발표자는 한 번의 설명으로 청중들이 쉽게 이해할 수 있도록 말해야 한다. 따라서 필요에 따라서 정보를 쉽게 단순화하여 전달해야 한다.

5.1 Simplify information using it's a kind of, it's a type of
정보를 단순화하여 전달하는 방법

The phrases **It's a kind of**, **It's a type of**, can be used to simplify the material you are presenting. The word **basically** can be added to these expressions like this. **Basically, it's a kind of**, **Basically, it's a type of**. The word **basically** is used to indicate that what follows is a simplification.

학회 발표에서는 시간이 제한되어 있어서 논문과 달리 모든 내용을 상세하게 설명할 수 없다. 자세하게 설명하지 않아도 되는 내용은 단순화하여 쉽게 전달하도록 한다. 이런 경우에는 **It's a kind of ~ / It's a type of ~**(일종의 ~ / ~와 같은), **basically**(간단히 말하면 ~ / 기본적으로는 ~) 등의 표현으로 정보가 단순화되었음을 나타낼 수 있다.

Script(실험 재료를 단순화하여 설명하는 예시)

To measure levels of pollution, we launched balloons with sensors at a height of 100 meters. These were attached to stakes in the ground with the white material seen in the photograph. Basically, the material is made of nylon. It's a kind of fishing line that was developed specifically for this purpose.

In the above example, using the words **basically** and **it's a kind of**, the presenter avoids a detailed explanation of the material used in the experiments to **save time** and **simplify the explanation**.

위의 예에서는 실험에 사용한 재료에 관해 자세한 설명은 생략하고 **basically**와 **it's a kind of ~**의 표현으로 간단하게 설명한다. 이렇게 하면 설명에 걸리는 시간을 줄일 수 있고, 청중도 이해하기 쉽다.

간단히 말해서 ~입니다.

- **Basically, the material is made of** nylon.
- **It's a kind of** fishing line.
- **It's a type of** fishing line made of nylon.
- **Basically, it's a kind of** fishing line made of nylon.
- **I won't go into details**. **Basically, it's a kind of / type of** fishing line made of nylon.

마지막 예문처럼 **I won't go into details**(**won't**는 **will not**의 단축형)의 한 문장으로 압축하여, 자세한 내용은 언급하지 않고 간단하게 줄일 수 있다.

In the last example, the expression **I won't go into details** signals a simplification.

5.2 Simplifying the material presented with in other words
바꾸어 말하는 방법 / 요약하여 말하는 방법

The expression **in other words** is a useful way of simplifying or summarizing a detailed explanation or a technical term.

Script(바꾸어 말하기의 예시)

Notice what happens with the adipic acid. The first proton is more like the proton in acetic acid. In other words, the P-K-A has gone up relative to the P-K-A of succinic acid.

To make your presentation as clear as possible, it is necessary to simplify the material presented. This not only saves time, but also makes it easier for the audience to follow. The most frequently used expression is **in other words**. A similar expression is **to put it simply**. The word **basically** can also be used.

In other words는 '다시 말하면', '요컨대'라는 뜻으로, 알기 쉽게 바꾸어 말할 때 사용하는 표현이다. 이러한 목적으로 **to put it simply** 또는 **basically**를 사용할 수도 있다.

바꾸어 말하면 / 요컨대, ~입니다.

- **In other words,** the results we got seem to have a high degree of reliability.
- **In other words,** there is a lot of essential bacteria that is required if we want to degrade plastic in soil.
- **To put it simply,** online questionnaires are a simple way of collecting feedback.
- **Basically,** online questionnaires are a simple way of collecting feedback.

Common errors ― 흔히 하는 실수

✕ In other *word*, it has a high degree of reliability.
○ In other **words**, it has a high degree of reliability.

The phrase **in other words** is always in the plural. This means you cannot say ***in other word*** with no **s**.

In other words라고 할 때 words는 항상 복수형으로 사용해야 한다. *In other word*는 잘못된 표현이다.

5.3 How to rephrase your explanation with What I mean is, What I want to say is, So, I mean that, My point is that, I'll just rephrase that 쉬운 말로 바꾸어 말하는 방법

The word **rephrase** means to **say something in different words so that it is clearer**. Rephrasing what you have said will help the audience to follow the points you are making.

동사 rephrase는 '다시 말하다'라는 뜻으로, 요점을 쉽게 표현할 때 사용한다.

바꾸어 말하면 / 즉, 요점은 ~입니다.

- **What I mean is that** by using this material, battery performance improves.
- **What I want to say is that** by using this material, battery performance improves.
- **So, I mean that** by using this material, battery performance improves.
- **My point is that** by using this material, battery performance improves.
- **I'll just rephrase that.** Using this material, battery performance improves.

요점을 강조하려면 다음과 같은 표현을 사용하는 것이 좋다.

In the last example, **rephrase** is a verb.

Note In some cases, such as the question and answer session, you may need to return to something you said and rephrase it. You can use the expressions presented in section 5.3. However, the sentences **should be in the past tense**. Here are some examples.

- **What I meant was**
- **What I wanted to say was**
- **My point was that**
- **The point I was making was**

+ a short explanation.

If you use the word **rephrase** as a verb, here is an useful example.

- **I would like to rephrase what I said about (topic).**

왼쪽의 표현은 발표 중간이나 질의응답 시간에 발표 내용을 되돌아보는 상황에서 사용할 수 있다. 이 경우에 왼쪽의 표현은 반드시 과거형으로 사용해야 한다. 예: What I meant was ~, What I wanted to say was ~, My point was that ~, The point I was making was ~. 동사 rephrase를 사용하는 경우는 I would like to rephrase what I said about (topic)이라고 표현하는 것이 좋다.

6 Giving an estimate using the words about, approximately, in the region of, typical, typically, basically
자세하게 언급하지 않고 대략적인 수치 / 일반론을 말하는 방법

In this section, I introduce useful words and expressions for giving an estimate and simplifying your explanation.

6.1 About, approximately, in the region of
대략적인 수치를 말한다

In some cases, you will not be able to give a precise number or value, because you do not have the data, or because you want to save time and avoid a detailed explanation. Giving an estimate is not a problem as long as you make it clear that the figure is only an estimate. You can use these expressions to **indicate that the information is an estimate.**

구두발표에서 수치를 설명할 때 정확한 데이터가 없거나 세세한 수치를 읽을 시간이 없는 경우에는 대략적인 수치를 제시한다. 이렇게 표현하면 그 수치가 추정치라는 것이 분명하게 나타날 수 있다.

● **About** 대략, 약

- Reported values are **about 10 percent.**

수치가 대략적인 값임을 나타내려면 왼쪽 표현 가운데 하나를 수치 앞에 붙여서 말한다.

● **Approximately** 대략, 약

- Reported values are **approximately 10 percent.**
- The reduction in time is **approximately 15 minutes.**

● **In the region of** 대략, 약, 거의 ~ 정도

- The yearly yield is **in the region of** one million tons.
- The reaction time is **in the region of** 4 to 5 minutes.
- Reported values are **in the region of** 10 percent.

6.2 How to use the words typical and typically to make a general statement that will simplify your explanation
일반적인 수치를 말하는 방법

Use the words typical or typically to give the audience a rough idea of **a number**, **amount**, **quantity**, or **time**. These words are useful because you can avoid detailed explanations by focusing on the main points, or giving an estimate. They are also an easy way of **giving a short answer** in the question and answer session.

아래의 예시처럼, 어떤 수량이 조건의 차이에 따라 다양한 값을 취할 수 있는 경우에는 상세한 설명은 생략하고 가장 일반적인 값만을 소개할 수가 있다. 이때에는 typical 또는 typically라는 용어로 표현한다. 이 방법은 질의응답 때에도 유용하다.

● Typical 일반적인/전형적인(형용사)

Script(수치가 다양하게 나타날 수 있음을 설명한 후에 일반적인 수치를 말하는 예시)

The yield from this experiment depends on the location and a few other variables. A typical yield is from 5 to 10 percent.

일반적으로는/보통은 ○○(수치 등)입니다.

Examples

- **A typical yield is 5 to 10 percent.**
- **A typical duration would be 24 hours.**

The word **typical** is usually followed by a noun such as **yield** or **duration**. For example, **a typical yield is 10 per cent**, **a typical duration is 24 hours**, **a typical increase is 10 grams**.

Typical은 형용사이며, 그 뒤에는 수량을 나타내는 명사[예: yield(비율), duration(지속 시간), increase(증가량)]가 이어진다.

There are two grammar patterns.
1. **A typical yield is**
2. **A typical yield would be**

The most frequent pattern is **a typical yield is**. There is no difference in meaning between these expressions, but the

A typical ~ is도 A typical ~ would be와 뜻은 거의 같지만, A typical ~ is 쪽이 좀 더 직접적인 표현이다.

expression **A typical yield would be** is slightly less direct than **A typical yield is**.

Useful expressions are:

- **A typical yield** is **in the region of** 10 to 20 percent.
  approximately
  about
  around

- **A typical yield** is 100,000 tons.
  duration is 10 minutes.
  increase is 15 percent.
  distance is several kilometres.
  weight is 15 kilos.
  temperature is 25 degrees.

● Typically 일반적으로/전형적으로/보통은(부사)

The word **typically** is frequently used at the beginning of a sentence, but can also be used after a verb. Please note that **typically** is often used in the question and answer session when presenters want to give a **quick, short answer** that involves numbers, time, amount, duration or quantity.

Typically는 부사이며, 보통은 문장 앞에 사용하지만, 동사(be 동사 포함) 뒤에 사용할 수도 있다.

Typically는 질의응답 시간에 수치에 관한 질문에 간단하게 대답할 때 자주 사용한다.

보통은/일반적으로는 ○○(수치 등)입니다.

- **Typically**, cell culture time is 2 to 3 days.
- Cell culture time is **typically** 2 to 3 days.
- **Typically**, values are in the region of 5 to 10 percent.
- Values are **typically** in the region of 5 to 10 percent.

6.3 How to use the word basically to simplify your explanation
복잡한 내용을 단순화하여 설명하는 방법

The word **basically** is used for simplification, and makes it possible to avoid long and complicated explanations. It is also useful for handling difficult questions. Please note that basically is used in **oral and poster presentations, but not in academic papers**. Here are some examples.

Script(복잡한 과정을 단순화하여 간단히 설명하고 있는 예시)

This process is quite complicated. Basically, the materials are stacked on top of each other with adhesive added at each level for stability. This means that stability increases by over 10 percent.

Here, the presenter avoids a detailed description of a complicated process. The word **basically** is used to **introduce a simplified explanation that is short and avoids unnecessary explanation**. In this example, the expression **this means** signals the start of a brief explanation.

구두발표나 질의응답을 할 때 복잡한 내용을 길게 설명할 시간이 없으면 내용을 단순/간략하게 하여 문장 앞부분에 basically(간단히 말하면, / 기본적으로는 ~)를 붙여 말하는 것이 좋다.

간단히 말하면,/기본적으로, ~입니다.

- **Basically,** this system can be used in any situation.
- **Basically,** we take a number of cells, immerse them in solution for 24 hours and measure their activity levels.

Basically라는 표현은 구두발표나 포스터 발표에서만 사용하고, 논문을 작성할 때에는 사용할 수 없으니 주의해야 한다.

In example 2, the presenter uses the word **basically** to indicate that the following short explanation is a simplification of a complicated process.

두 번째 예문은, 문장 앞에 basically라는 표현을 함으로써 그 뒤에 이어지는 실험 순서에 관한 설명이 단순화된 것임(실제로는 훨씬 복잡함)을 나타낸다.

7 Skipping information and focusing on the main points
요점 설명에 집중하고, 일부 설명은 생략하는 방법

If your slides have a lot of detailed information, you may need to skip some of it to save time and simplify your explanation.

7.1 When you need to skip some of the material on a slide
슬라이드의 일부 정보에 대한 설명을 생략한다

이 자료에 관한 설명은 생략하겠습니다.

- **I'll skip this data.**

슬라이드의 일부 자료/도표에 관한 설명을 생략한다면 왼쪽처럼 말하면 된다.

자세한 내용은 생략하겠습니다.

- This slide contains a lot of facts / figures / information / data / material. **I'll skip the detail / details.**
- There is a lot information here. **I'll skip the detail / details.**
- There is a lot of information here. **I won't / will not go into detail / details.**

Please note that both **detail** and **details** can be used. Also note the useful expression **to go into detail / details**. In the expression, **I'll skip the details**, the definite article is necessary. The expression, **I will not go into details**, has a two-word verb **go into**.

'자세한 내용은 생략한다'라고 말할 때 '자세(상세)'는 단수형 **detail**이든 복수형 **details**든 어느 쪽이든 사용할 수 있다. 구동사 **go into**를 사용하여 **I will not/won't go into details**라고 할 때는 the가 필요 없지만, **I'll skip the details**라고 할 때는 **the**가 있어야 한다.

7.2 When you need to skip a slide completely
일부 슬라이드는 건너뛴다

시간이 부족하여 이 슬라이드는 그냥 넘어가겠습니다.

- I'll skip this slide.
- I'm running out of time, so I'll skip this slide.
- I only have a few minutes left, so I'll skip this slide.
- Time is limited. So, I'm afraid I'll have to skip the next few slides.

일부 슬라이드를 통째로 건너뛸 때는 왼쪽과 같이 말하면 된다. 슬라이드 한 장을 건너뛸 때는 1~3번째 예문처럼, 슬라이드 여러 장을 건너뛸 때는 4번째 예문처럼 말한다.

7.3 When you need to skip details but want to focus on a few main points
상세한 설명은 생략하고 요점만 설명한다.

When there is a lot of information on your slide, you should focus on the main points to help the audience follow, and also to save time. You should remember that the audience will rapidly scan the information as you speak. You do not need to explain everything on the slide in detail.

구두발표에서는 청중이 슬라이드 전체를 한눈에 볼 수 있으므로 발표자가 그 정보를 말로 다 설명할 필요는 없다. 요점만 설명할 때는 다음 쪽의 표현을 사용한다.

Script(자료가 많아서 요점만 설명하겠다고 말하는 예시)

This table shows data collected from 7 different experiments. As you can see, the slide has a lot of information. So, I'll skip the details and focus on the main points, which are as follows: (explain the main points briefly).

자세한 내용은 생략하고 중요한 부분만 설명하겠습니다.

- **There is a lot of information here. So, I'll skip the details and look at** the main points, which are as follows: (explain the main points).
- **I'll skip the details and (just) mention** the important information / the key data.
- Here we have data from group 2, **I won't go into details, but the main point is** (explain the main point).

첫 번째 예문처럼 '요점은 다음과 같습니다'라고 말할 때는 as follows: (+ 요점 리스트)로 표현한다. 이 경우 follow는 동사이며 s를 붙여야 한다. 반면에, The following points라고 할 때는 *following*이 형용사이므로 여기에 s를 붙이지 않아야 한다.

Note How to use as follows and the following

1. **I'll skip the details and look at** the main points, which are **as follows:**

In this usage, it is important to have an s on the word follow. The expression as follows, is usually followed by a list. *As follow* is a common error.

2. **The following points are important.**

In this example, the pattern is **the following points**. There is no s on the word **following**. You cannot say, **The *followings* are important**. This is a common error where presenters confuse the two expressions. **As follows** and **the following**.

7.4 How to focus on the main points: Using I'll (just) focus on, I'll go over, I'll look at, I'll run through
요점을 간추려 설명한다

Script(요점만 설명한다는 말을 focus on ~으로 표현하는 예시)

In field experiments, we collected data on windspeed, precipitation and humidity at 16 sites over a period of 12 months. Here is the data. There is a lot of detailed information, so I'll just focus on the main points.

Focus on

- This slide is a bit busy, so, I'll focus on the main points / the key data.
- This slide is somewhat busy, so, I'll focus on the main points / the important information.
- There is a lot of information, so, I'll focus on the main points / the latest data.
- There's a lot of data here. I'll skip the details and focus on the main points.

"자세한 내용은 생략하고 요점만 설명하겠습니다."라고 말할 때는 왼쪽의 구동사 중에 하나를 활용한다.

Go over

- As you can see, there is a lot of data, so, I'll go over the main points.
- There is a lot of data here. So, I'll go over the main points.
- This slide is rather busy, so, I'll go over the important information.

Look at

- There is a lot of information here. I'll look at the most recent results.
- There is a lot of data here. I'll look at the results from experiment 2 only.

Run through

- There is a lot of information here. I'll run through the most important results.
- There is a lot of data here. I'll just run through the main points.

When you skip data / information and focus on important points, these verbs are frequently used.

- **There is a lot of data here.**
  I'll focus on the main points in this slide.
  go over
  look at
  run through
  concentrate on

Here are some expressions that are frequently used in combination with the above verbs.

- I'll (just) go over the main points.
  the most recent data.
  the most important data.
  the most important results.
  the most relevant data.
  the key data.
  the essential information.

여기에서 소개하는 구동사를 활용하여 '요점(만)을 설명한다'고 말할 때는 구동사 뒤에 '요점' 또는 '중요한 자료'의 내용을 이어서 말한다.

8 How to help the audience follow your presentation by using forward movement, backward movement, and reminders
다음에 언급할 내용을 예고하는 방법 / 앞에서 언급한 내용을 되짚어 보는 방법

In this section, I introduce useful sentences that will make it easy for the audience to follow the presentation.

Forward movement(앞쪽으로 이동=다음에 말할 내용에 대한 설명)와 backward movement(뒤쪽으로 이동=앞에서 말했던 내용을 되짚어 보기)를 활용하면 청중이 발표의 구성을 파악하기 쉽다.

8.1 Forward movement
다음에 말할 내용을 예고한다

You can help the audience follow your presentation by signaling forward movement. The examples below can be used to tell the audience what will happen in the next few minutes of the presentation. This helps people to understand the structure of your presentation.
These examples are for referring to information in the next slide.

~에 대해서는 다음 슬라이드에서 말씀드리겠습니다.

- So, the main issue is reliability. I'll talk about that in the next slide.
- So, the main issue is reliability. I'll focus on that in the next slide.
- So, the main issue is reliability. That is what I am going to talk about next.
- So, the main issue is reliability. That's my next point.

Forward movement(다음에 말할 내용에 대한 설명)에는 다음 슬라이드에서 말할 내용을 예고하거나, 다음 항목에서 말할 내용을 예고하는 경우가 있다.

These examples are for introducing information in the next section.

~에 대해서는 다음 항목에서 말씀드리겠습니다.

- I'll talk about the significance of this result in the next section.
- I'll look at the experimental data in the results.
- I'll come back to this point in the discussion.
- I'll mention this again in the materials and methods section.
- I'll return to this issue later.
- I'll introduce some more data on this topic later.
- I'll show you that information in a moment.
- I'll give you some more information about this shortly.

Commonly used verbs when introducing forward movement

- I'll talk about this issue in the next section / in the results / in part 2.
  explain
  say something about
  look at
  give you some data on
  give you some examples of
  introduce some more data on
- I'll show you that data / information / those results in the discussion.
- I'll come back to this issue in the next section.
- I'll return to this issue in part 3.

Commonly used expressions when introducing forward movement

- I'll talk about this issue in the next slide.
  in the next few slides.
  in the discussion.
  in a moment.
  in a few minutes.
  shortly.
  in the next section / in part 2.
  later.
  at the end of the presentation.

8.2 Backward movement
앞에서 말했던 내용을 되짚어 본다

In backward movement, you **remind the audience of information you have already covered**. This **improves the connectivity of the presentation** and **makes your presentation easier to follow and remember**.

Backward movement(앞에서 말했던 내용을 되짚어 보기)를 적절히 활용하면 앞뒤의 내용이 명확하게 연결되어 청중이 내용을 쉽게 이해할 수 있다.

How to briefly return to a point you have already made.

좀 전에 ~의 항목에서 말씀드린 것처럼, ~입니다.

- **As I mentioned in the background,** typical lifespans for this product are between 5 to 7 years.
- **As I said in the background,** typical lifespans for this product are between 5 to 7 years.
- **As I explained in the introduction,** typical lifespans for this product are between 5 to 7 years.
- **As I pointed out at the beginning of my talk,** typical lifespans for this product are between 5 to 7 years.
- **As I told you in part 1,** typical lifespans for this product are between 5 to 7 years.
- **As we saw in the previous slide,** this method also has medical applications.
- **As we saw previously,** this method also has medical applications.
- **Here is the data we saw in experiment 1.** And this is the new data from our most recent experiment. **As you can see,** there are some significant differences.

앞에서 언급한 내용을 되짚어 볼 때는 왼쪽 예시처럼 As I (+ 동사) in (+ 어느 항목), ~의 표현을 활용한다. 즉, '앞서 (어느 항목)에서 말씀드렸으며, (앞서 언급한 내용의 요약)입니다'라는 방식으로 말한다.

In the above example, the sentence, **Here is the data we saw in experiment 1**, is used to refer to previously presented material.

마지막 예문은 슬라이드에 두 가지 실험 결과(한 쪽은 앞서 설명한 내용, 다른 쪽은 새로 제시한 내용)를 함께 보여 줄 때, 앞서 설명한 내용을 레이저 포인터로 가리키면서 "이 쪽은 방금 말씀드린 내용입니다."라고 말하는 표현이다.

Verbs for **backward movement** are as follows in order of frequency:

As I mentioned, said, told you, explained, pointed out, As we saw

앞서 설명한 내용을 되짚어 볼 때는 왼쪽에 열거한 동사 중에 하나를 활용한다. **Mentioned** 또는 **said** 동사를 사용하는 경우에는 주어가 **I**가 되고, **saw** (**see**의 과거형)를 사용하는 경우에는 주어가 **we**가 되니 주의해야 한다.

> **Note** The expression, **As we saw** is a useful way of referring to something you have already said or shown the audience. It is usually used with these expressions. **As we saw in the introduction, background, materials and methods, last section, in experiment 1.**

Commonly used expressions for **backward movement** are as follows:

- As I mentioned **in the background,** battery performance improves.
  in the introduction,
  in the previous section,
  in part 1,
  previously,
  in the last section,
  a moment ago,
  a few minutes ago,
  just now,

언제 어디에서 설명한 내용인지 확인하는 표현을 하려면 **in the background** 또는 **in part 1**과 같이 어느 항목/슬라이드 번호를 말하거나, **a few minutes ago**(몇 분 전)처럼 말한다.

How to use the expression go back to for backward movement.

~의 항목에서 말씀드린 내용을 다시 되짚어 보려고 합니다.

- I'd like to go back to what I said about medical applications.
- I want to go back to the introduction.
- I'll just go back to the results and mention applications.
- I'm going to go back to the experimental setup and remind you of the major differences between these systems.

왼쪽처럼, 구동사 go back to(거슬러 올라가다)를 사용할 수도 있다.

8.3 How to refer back to information already presented using the word remind
중요 사항을 다시 설명할 때 사용하는 표현: remind와 reminder

In order to stress the important information in your presentation, it is necessary to remind people of the main points you have already covered.

Script(중요 사항을 다시 설명하는 상황을 동사 remind로 표현하는 예)

Ok, so I'd just like to remind you of the material / data / ground / information we have covered. We modified the system with additional battery power. After further tests, we found that processing speed, reliability and usability went up.

In some cases, presenters will support their explanation with notes on a slide like these.

- system was modified using additional battery power
- processing speed went up
- reliability and usability improved

중요한 내용을 돌이켜 생각해 보겠습니다.

- I'd just like to remind you of the material / data / ground / information we have covered.

● Remind

- I'd (just) like to remind you of the main points so far. (+ short summary)
- I want to remind you of the points I made in the last section. (+ short summary)
- I'd (just) like to remind you of the results. (+ short summary)
- This is (just) to remind you of the main points I made in the last section. (+ short summary)
- I want to remind you of the key data. (+ short summary)

● Reminder

- This is (just) a quick reminder of the main points so far. + List of main points.
- This is a reminder of the main points. We found that temperature increased, and that the reaction was longer. We also found that the flexibility of the samples improved.

중요한 내용을 다시 설명하겠다는 표현을 할 때는 동사 remind(생각나게 하다)와 명사 reminder(생각나게 하는 것)를 사용한다. Remind는 I'd (just) like to remind you of the main points (+ 중요한 내용의 요약)의 형태로, Reminder는 This is (just) a reminder of the main points. We found (+ 중요한 내용의 요약)의 방식으로 활용한다. 요약한 내용을 말로 전달하는 방식 외에도 슬라이드의 항목마다 요점을 표시하면 효과적이다.

Common errors – 흔히 하는 실수

X As I *said you*, reliability is an issue.
O As I said, reliability is an issue.
O As I told you in the introduction, reliability is an issue.

In backward movement, the word said is frequently used. After the word said, *you* is not necessary. However, if you use the word told, it is necessary to use you. For example, As I told you, degradation is an issue.

'(조금 전에) 말씀드린 것처럼'이라고 말할 때, said라는 동사를 사용한다면 뒤에 you를 붙이지 말아야 하고(*As I said you*는 잘못된 표현), told라는 동사를 사용한다면 뒤에 you를 붙여서 말해야 한다(As I told you가 맞는 표현).

X As I *talked*, cost is an issue.
O As I mentioned / said / explained / told you / pointed out, cost is an issue.
O As we saw, cost is an issue.

The verb talk cannot be used like this. *As I talked*. However, talked about can be used in the following examples, where it is preceded by in the previous/last slide. For example, In the introduction, in the previous/last slide, I talked about cost.
I talked about cost in the introduction, in the previous/last slide.

'(조금 전에) 말씀드린 것처럼'이라는 표현을 As I (+동사), ~의 방식으로 말할 때는 said 또는 mentioned 등의 동사를 사용하지만, *As I talked*라고 한다면 이는 잘못된 표현이다. I talked about ~라고 말하려면 그 앞에 In the Introduction 또는 In the previous slide 등의 표현이 함께 있어야 하니, 주의해야 한다.

X As I *spoke*, cost is an issue.
O As I said, cost is an issue.

In this case, spoke cannot be used with the expression As I + verb.
However, spoke about can be used in the following pattern. In the introduction, I spoke about applications. In this case, spoke about or talked about can both be used. But the frequency of talked about is much higher than spoke about.

*As I talked*와 마찬가지로 *As I spoke*도 잘못된 표현이다. I talked about의 경우처럼 In the introduction, I spoke about 방식으로 말할 수는 있겠지만, 이 경우에도 일반적으로 spoke가 아닌 talked를 사용하는 것이 좋다.

9 Focusing on information on the slide
청중에게 슬라이드의 특정 부분을 주목해 달라고 요청하는 표현

It is necessary to guide the audience through the information on the slide, focusing on key information using **I'd like to focus on**, **Let's take a look at**, **Let's look at** and **Please look at**.

슬라이드에 포함된 여러 정보 가운데 특히 어디를 주목해 달라고 요청하거나, 무엇이 중요한지 등을 청중에게 표현해야 하는 상황이 있다.

9.1 Draw the attention of the audience to important information
슬라이드에서 특히 주목할 부분을 지정한다

Script(슬라이드에서 주목할 부분을 지정한 후, 거기에서 무엇을 알 수 있는지 설명하는 예시)

I'd like to focus on the table on the right. It includes data on precipitation. As you can see, September is the wettest month.

This is a 2-step move. In step 1, the presenter focuses on a particular part of the slide with the sentence, **I'd like to focus on** topic. In part 2, the presenter explains the data with the sentence, **As you can see**, September is the wettest month.

위의 예시에서는 청중이 도표를 주목해 주기 바란다는 표현을 **I'd like to focus on** ~이라고 말한 다음, 그 도표에서 무엇을 읽을 수 있는지 **As you can see**의 방식으로 설명한다.

~에 주목해 주십시오. 이 도표/데이터에서 ~인 것을 알 수 있습니다.

- **I'd like to focus on** the table on the right. **As you can see,** there is a reduction in weight.
- **Let's take a look at** the experimental setup. **As you have probably noticed,** there is a reduction in size.
- **Let's look at** the bar chart. **As you have probably seen,** rates are fairly consistent.
- **Please look at** the precipitation data. **As you have probably noted,** June has become progressively drier.

청중에게 특정 부분에 주목해 봐달라는 요청을 할 때 I'd like to focus on ~ 외에도 Let's take a look at ~, Let's look at ~, Please look at ~ 등의 표현을 쓸 수도 있다.

Common errors — 흔히 하는 실수

× *Please see this figure.*
○ **I'd like to focus on** this figure.
○ **Let's take a look at** this figure.
○ **Let's look at** this figure.

The expression, **Please see this figure,** is incorrect. It would be possible to say, **Please look at.** The most frequently used expression in this case is, **I'd like to focus on.**

'~를 좀 봐주시기 바랍니다'를 *Please* see라고 표현하면 안 된다. Please ~를 사용한다면 Please look at ~으로 말해야 한다. 이 경우에 일반적으로 I'd like to focus on ~이라고 말하는 것이 가장 좋다.

9.2 How to use the word if to focus on information on the slide
주목할 부분/요점을 표현하는 방법(1): if

The word **if** is frequently used in oral presentations, particularly when explaining information on a slide. **If** is used to draw the attention of the audience to important information on the slide.

> If를 문장 앞에 두고 '~을 보시면'이라고 표현하면서 주목할 부분을 언급할 수 있다.

~을 보시면 ~인 것을 알 수 있습니다.

- **If you look at this red line, you will see that** degradation increases rapidly after day 3.
- **If you look at this data, you will notice that** degradation increases rapidly after day 3.
- **If you look at the results for experiment 3, you will see** a sudden increase in dopamine.
- **If we look at the reaction site, we can see** that changing the catalyst causes a dramatic reaction.

> If를 사용하는 경우는 왼쪽 예문처럼, **If you/we look at (+ 주목할 부분), you will see/notice/observe/find (+ 그 부분에서 알 수 있는 내용)** 등의 방식으로 말한다.

If is usually positioned at the start of the sentence and is used with the verb **look at**. The pattern is as follows: **If you / we look at**. The second part of the same sentence starts with **you will see** / **notice** / **observe** / **find**.

Common errors ─ 흔히 하는 실수

✕ If we **see** figure 2, the temperature increase is clear.
○ If we **look at** figure 2, we can see that the temperature increase is clear.

✕ If you **see** the samples carefully, you can see small fractures in the surface.
○ If you **look at** the samples carefully, you can see small fractures in the surface.

> **Please look at** ~의 경우처럼 **if**를 사용할 때는 동사를 **see**가 아니라 **look at** ~을 사용해야 한다.

The word **if** is usually used with **look at**. It is not used with **see**.

9.3 Using the words interestingly and interesting to focus on important information
주목할 부분/요점을 표현하는 방법(2): interestingly, interesting

A flat presentation is difficult to follow because the presenter does not stress the main points. In other words, there is no hierarchy of main points and the presentation is monotonous. The words interestingly and interesting help to emphasize the main points and get the attention of the audience.

발표자가 단조롭게 발표를 이어나가면 청중은 무엇이 중요한 정보인지 이해하기 어렵다. 요점을 강조하는 표현을 적절히 활용하여 발표가 단조롭지 않도록 변화를 주어야 한다.

흥미롭게도/재미있는 것은, ~입니다.

- Interestingly, most of these results show/suggest that temperature rises from day 2.
- Interestingly, rates of degradation level off after week 2.
- It is interesting that temperature rises from day 2.
- The interesting point here is that the temperature rises from day 2.
- What is interesting (here / in this case / in this experiment) is that the temperature rises from day 2.

왼쪽은 interestingly(부사) 또는 interesting(형용사)을 사용하여 요점을 표현하는 예시이다.

9.4 Using the word note to focus on important information
주목할 부분/요점을 표현하는 방법(3): note

In the following examples, the word **note** is used to focus on important information.

Script(One thing to note is ~를 사용하여 주목할 부분을 표현하는 예시)

So here we have a lot of data on reliability. One thing to note is the sudden decrease at this point. This indicates a change in the structure of the material.

~에 주목해 주시기 바랍니다. / 주목할 부분은 ~입니다.

- **One thing to note is** the sudden decrease at this point.
- **Please note** the sudden decrease at this point. **This indicates a change in** the structure of the material.
- **You will note that there is a** sudden decrease at this point. **This indicates a change in** the structure of the material.
- **As you have (already) probably noted**, there is a sudden decrease at this point. **This indicates** that the molecules are in an excited state.
- **I guess that many of you will have (already) noted that** there is a sudden decrease at this point. **This shows** that the molecules are in an excited state.
- **Many of you will have (already) noted that** there is a sudden decrease at this point. **This means** that the molecules are in an excited state.
- **Of note is** a sudden decrease in reliability. **This indicates a change** in the structure of the material.

위의 예에서는 동사 note(주목하다/깨닫다)를 사용하여 도표에서 주목할 부분을 강조하고, 그것이 무엇을 나타낼지 This indicates ~로 설명하고 있다.

As you have (already) probably noted 또는 Many of you will have (already) noted that ~의 표현으로, '여러분께서 이미 알고 계신 것처럼'이라고 말해도 괜찮다.

9.5 How to focus on the main points using the words, stress, emphasize, point out, and draw your attention to
주목할 부분/요점을 표현하는 방법(4): stress, emphasize, point out, draw your attention to

In the examples presented here, the words **stress**, **emphasize**, **point out** and **draw your attention to** are used to focus on the main points.

Stress, emphasize, point out, draw your attention to 등의 동사는 요점을 강조할 때 활용한다.

~라는 것을 강조하고 싶습니다. / 중요한 것은 ~입니다.

- **I'd like to stress that** although the amount of nutrients in the soil increased, the yield did not decline.
- **I'd like to emphasize that** although the amount of nutrients in the soil increased, the yield did not decline.
- **I'd like to point out that** although the amount of nutrients in the soil increased, the yield did not decline.
- **I want to draw your attention to** the increase in the amount of nutrients in the soil. It means that the yield did not decline.
- **I'd like to draw your attention to** this red line. It shows the yield.
- **I want to draw your attention to the fact that** although the amount of nutrients in the soil increased, the yield did not decline.

Note The expression **draw your attention** to is followed by to. Common patterns are **draw your attention to something** and **draw your attention to the fact that**.

- **I want to draw your attention to** figure 1.
- **I'd like to draw your attention to** the increase in temperature.
- **I want to draw your attention to the fact that** the yield did not increase.
- **I'd like to draw your attention to the fact that** the performance improved.

Draw your attention은 I want to / would like to draw your attention to (~에 주목하길 바란다)의 방식으로 말한다. 강조하고 싶은 대상이 문장일 때는 to 뒤에 the fact that (+ 문장)으로 연결하여 '~라는 사실에 주목해 주시길 바란다'로 말한다.

9.6 How to use the words point/points to avoid a flat presentation
주목할 부분/요점을 표현하는 방법(5): point/points

I see a lot of presentations that are generally good, but too flat. You can avoid a flat presentation by using these expressions, which focus on key information.

핵심은 ~입니다.

- My point is that after these simple modifications, performance improves dramatically.

● Point 핵심/요점(단수형)

- My point is that after these simple modifications, performance improves dramatically.
- The point is that after these simple modifications, performance improves dramatically.
- The main point is that after these simple modifications, performance improves dramatically.
- The key point is that after these simple modifications, performance improves dramatically.
- The point I am making is that after these simple modifications, performance improves dramatically.

● Points 핵심/요점(복수형)

- The key points are as follows. After changes to the system, performance, reliability and speed improved.
- Here are the key points. After changes to the system, performance, reliability and speed improved.
- These are the key points. After changes to the system, performance, reliability and speed improved.
- These are the main points. After changes to the system, performance, reliability and speed improved.

9.7 How to use the words issue/issues to avoid a flat presentation
주목할 부분/요점을 표현하는 방법(6): issue/issues

~는 중대한 과제입니다.

- The main issue is the stability of the system.

● Issue 과제/문제(단수형)

- The main issue is the stability of the system.
- So, the biggest issue is the stability of the system.
- Stability is a big issue in this field.
- Stability is a big issue in this type of experiment.
- Another issue is stability.

● Issues 과제/문제(복수형)

- One of the key issues is the choice of catalyst.
- There are several issues with the stability of the system.
- There are a number of issues with the stability of the system.
- There are several issues here. Reliability, cost and performance.

Note Presenters sometimes use the following sentence. *This is a big problem*. It is grammatically correct, but a little too direct and somewhat informal. I would change it to, This is a significant issue or This is a serious issue. The word issue is more academic than problem. Another frequent error is the use of the following sentences: *That does not matter. It does not matter*. The following sentences are more academic and suitable for a presentation.

- That is not an issue.
- It is not an issue.
- Stability is not an issue.

'중대한 문제'를 *big problem*이라고 표현하면 정중한 학회 발표에서는 실례이므로 피해야 한다. 따라서 problem이 아니라 issue를 사용하고, significant issue 또는 serious issue로 표현한다.

마찬가지로, '문제가 되지 않는다'를 *That does not matter* 또는 *It does not matter*라고 표현하는 것도 학회 발표에서는 피하는 것이 좋다. 이 경우에도 issue를 사용해 That is not an issue 등으로 표현한다.

10 Focusing on results
결과와 고찰을 설명하는 방법

10.1 Signal the start of your explanation of the data using a question
결과에 대한 고찰을 시작한다

Here the presenter is moving from description of the results to explanation of them. A question is used to signal the movement from **description** to **explanation**.

조사 또는 실험의 결과를 설명할 때는 먼저 어떤 결과를 얻었는지를 기술(**description**)한 후에, 그 결과가 무엇을 의미하는지, 그 결과로부터 어떤 결론을 도출할 수 있는지 등을 고찰하는 순서로 설명(**explanation**)을 이어간다. 왼쪽의 의문문을 활용하여 **Description**에서 **explanation**으로 넘어가는 표현을 삽입하면 발표가 단조로워지는 것을 막을 수 있다.

이 결과는 무엇을 의미하는 것일까요?

- **What do these results mean?**
- **What do these results tell us about** the mechanism?
- **What is the significance of** these results?
- **What can we conclude from** these results?
- **What do these figures tell us about** productivity?
- **What does this graph tell us about** productivity?
- **How can we interpret** this data?

10.2 Introducing results
결과를 요약하여 소개한다

Here I show some examples of how to introduce results.

Script(결과를 요약하여 전달하는 예시)

① So, in this slide, I have summarized the main results I presented in this section. ② With the modified device, using magnesium alloys, we achieved a significant reduction in power consumption. ③ At the same time, we saw an increase in efficiency. ④ In addition, the reliability of the device increased. ⑤ One remaining issue is the difficulty of shaping alloys into new forms. ⑥ We found that through heat treatment, both the microstructure and mechanical properties can be controlled. ⑦ We also noted increases in quality, reliability and strength.

Key sentences

1. Signal that you will introduce the results
결과를 말씀드리겠다고 언급한다

주요 결과를 요약하여 보여 드리겠습니다.

- **So, in this slide, I have summarized the main results I presented in this section.**

먼저, 결과를 요약한 슬라이드를 보여 주면서 다음과 같이 말하면 된다.

Examples

- Here is a summary of the main results.
- I'll just go over the main results.
- Here I have listed the key results for this section.

2. State results 1 결과를 말한다(1)

~라는 결과를 얻었습니다.

- With the modified device, using magnesium alloys, we achieved a significant reduction in power consumption.

Examples

- We obtained a significant reduction in power consumption.
- We got a significant reduction in power consumption.
- There was a significant reduction in power consumption.

'결과를 얻었다'를 표현하는 동사는 achieved 또는 obtained가 일반적이고, got을 사용하면 격식이 좀 떨어지는 느낌을 준다. 맨 아래의 예문처럼 There was ~로 표현하는 방식도 간단하면서 무난하다.

The verbs achieved and obtained are formal. The verb got is informal. The last example has a simple pattern. There was a significant reduction in power.

3. State results 2 결과를 말한다(2)

또 ~라는 결과도 함께 얻었습니다.

- At the same time, we saw an increase in efficiency.

Examples

- We also observed an increase in efficiency.
- There was also an increase in efficiency.
- Another thing we saw was that performance improved.

결과를 덧붙여 말할 때는 at the same time(동시에), also, in addition 등의 표현을 활용한다. Another thing we saw/noted was ~라고 말할 수도 있다.

4. Additional results 추가적인 결과를 말한다

아울러, ~도 확인하였습니다.

- In addition, the reliability of the device increased.

Examples

- There was also an increase in reliability.
- Another thing we noted was an increase in reliability.
- Another thing we saw was an increase in reliability.

5. Refer to issues 과제에 대해 언급한다

남은 과제는 ~입니다.

- One remaining issue is the difficulty of shaping alloys into new forms.

Examples

- An outstanding issue is the difficulty of shaping alloys into new forms.
- Another issue is the difficulty of shaping alloys into new forms.
- We are still working on the issue of shaping alloys into new forms.
- One problem is the difficulty of shaping alloys into new forms.

이미 말한 결과(2~4에서 설명한 결과)로는 해결되지 않은 과제에 관해 언급한다. '과제/문제'는 보통 issue로 표현한다.

6. Refer to solution 과제에 대한 해결책을 제시한다

~함으로써, ~할 수 있었습니다.

- We found that through heat treatment, both the microstructure and mechanical properties can be controlled.

Examples

- Through heat treatment, we can control the microstructure and mechanical properties.
- It is possible to control the microstructure and mechanical properties using heat treatment.
- We got around this problem by using heat treatment to control properties.
- We got over this problem by using heat treatment to control properties.

5에서 언급한 과제의 해결책을 제시한다. Through ~, we can ~(~에 의해 ~할 수 있었다)의 형태를 사용하거나, get around 또는 get over('넘어간다', '극복한다'라는 뜻) 등의 구동사를 활용하여 표현한다.

7. Additional results 추가하여 결과를 말한다

또, ~도 확인하였습니다.

- We also noted increases in quality, reliability and strength.

Examples

- There were also increases in quality, reliability, and strength.

10.3 Stating that data is not included
포함되지 않은 데이터가 있음을 언급한다

In some cases, you will need to state that data is not included.

~의 데이터는 여기에 포함되지 않습니다.

- That is the data from experiments 1 and 2. We actually did one other experiment, **but that data is not included here**.
- **That data is not included.**
- **I did not include that data.**
- **That data is not shown.**
- **There were some other results that I have not included here.**
- **There was/were some other data that I have not included here.**

결과를 나타내는 도표에는 데이터 중의 일부가 포함되어 있지 않을 수 있으므로, 이 경우에는 왼쪽과 같이 표현한다.

10.4 When the reason for something is unknown or unclear: Using the expressions We don't know why, We are not sure why, We don't know the reason for, The reason for X is not clear, The reason for X is unclear 원인이 명확하지 않은 부분에 관해 언급한다

In some cases, you will not be able to explain something. Here are some useful expressions.

~의 원인은 분명하지 않습니다.

- **We (still) don't know why** the reaction was unsuccessful.
- **We are not sure why** the reaction was unsuccessful.
- **We are not sure why there was** a sudden increase in temperature.
- **We don't know the reason for** the sudden increase in temperature.

결과에 대해 고찰을 할 때는 왜 그러한 결과를 얻었는지 설명해야 한다. 하지만 원인을 확실하게 설명할 수 없는 경우라면 왼쪽처럼 설명한다.

- **The reason for** the sudden increase in temperature **is not clear**.
- **The reason for** the sudden increase in temperature **is unclear**.

10.5 Stating that research on a topic is ongoing: Using the verbs checking, looking at, working on, investigating
연구를 계속 진행하고 있다는 점에 대해 언급한다

In this example, the presenter starts by saying that the reason for something is unknown, and then states that research on the topic is ongoing.

~의 원인은 모릅니다.
이 부분에 대해서는 지금도 계속 연구하고 있습니다.

- We are not sure why the reaction was unsuccessful. **We are still checking** that point.
- We are not sure why the reaction was unsuccessful. **We are still looking at** that issue.
- We are not sure why the reaction was unsuccessful. **We are still working on** that issue.
- We are not sure why the reaction was unsuccessful. **We are still investigating** that issue/point.

원인을 밝히기 위해 계속 연구하고 있다면 현재진행형으로 표현하는 것이 좋다.

Other reasons for not being able to explain something.

~의 원인은 모릅니다. 그것은 이번 결과가 ~였기 때문입니다.

- We don't know the reason for that. **Results were inconclusive.**
- We don't know the reason for that. **Results were difficult to interpret.**
- We can't give a concrete figure. **Results were mixed.**
- We can't really say anything about that issue. **Results were not significant.**

왼쪽처럼, 원인을 설명할 수 없는 이유를 언급하는 것도 좋은 방법이다[예: inconclusive(이 결과로는 결론을 내릴 수 없다), difficult to interpret(결과를 해석하기 어렵다), mixed(상반된 결론이 나올 수 있는 결과가 혼재되어 있다), not significant(유의차가 없다)].

10.6 Giving a reason: Using due to, because of, caused by, the reason for, the result of
원인을 설명한다

In many cases, it will be necessary to explain why something happens. Here are some examples:

Script(어떠한 결과를 얻었는지 → 그 원인은 무엇인지의 순서로 설명하는 예시)

As you can see, there was an increase in temperature on day 4 of the experiment. This was due to interaction between molecules.

• due to, because of, caused by

- **This was because of** interaction between molecules.
- **This was caused by** interaction between molecules.

원인을 명확하게 설명할 수 있는 경우에는 왼쪽 표현 중에 하나를 활용하여 설명한다.

• The reason for

- **The reason for this was** interaction between molecules.

• The result of, a result of, as a result of

- This was **the result of** interaction between molecules.
- This was **a result of** interaction between molecules.
- This was **as a result of** interaction between molecules.

The result of ~, a result of ~, as a result of ~ 등은 거의 같은 의미로 사용한다.

> **Note** The expressions **the result of, a result of, as a result of** have the same meaning, but the grammatical patterns are slightly different.

Common errors — 흔히 하는 실수

✕ ***The reason of*** the increase in temperature is interaction between molecules.

○ **The reason for** the increase in temperature is interaction between molecules.

The correct preposition to use with the word **reason** is **for**. You cannot say ***The reason of***. The correct pattern is as follows: **The reason for X is Y**.

'~ 결과의 근거'를 ***The reason of*** ~라고 표현하면 안 된다. **Reason**의 뒤에 이어지는 전치사는 ***of***가 아니라 **for**이니 주의해야 한다.

10.7 Giving a possible reason for something using the expressions: We think that, / We guess that, 추측하는 원인에 관해 말한다

Here, the presenter states that the **reason is not known**, but also **gives a possible explanation** that is introduced with the expressions **we think that** or **we guess that**. The sentence has two steps.

1. **We don't know the reason for X**
2. **but we think it was due to Y.**

This sentence pattern can be particularly useful in the question and answer session when handling a difficult question.

~의 원인은 정확히 모릅니다만, 저희는 ~에 의한 것이 아닐까 추측하고 있습니다.

- **We don't know the reason for** the difficulties in shaping alloys into new forms, **but we think that it was due to** a lack of heat control.

분명하게 말할 수는 없지만 추정하는 어떤 원인이 있는 경우에는 왼쪽과 같이 '원인은 모릅니다' → but → '~라고 생각합니다(we think/guess that ~)'의 형태로 설명하면 좋다. 이 표현 방법은 질의응답 시간에 활용하면 특히 좋다.

● We think that it was due to / We think that it was because of

- **We don't know the reason for** the difficulties in shaping alloys into new forms, **but we think that it was due to** a lack of heat control.
- **We don't know the reason for** the difficulties in shaping alloys into new forms, **but we think that it was because of** a lack of heat control.

● We guess that it was due to / We guess that it was because of

- **We don't know the reason for** the difficulties in shaping alloys into new forms, **but we guess that it was due to** a lack of heat control.
- **We don't know the reason for** the difficulties in shaping alloys into new forms, **but we guess that it was because of** a lack of heat control.
- **We are not sure why this happened, but we guess that it was due to** a buildup of pressure.
- **We are not sure why** the sample degraded, **but we guess that it was due to** exposure to sunlight. **There may have been other reasons.**

마지막 예문처럼 '(~라고 생각합니다) 하지만, 다른 원인도 있을 수 있습니다'라고 말할 때는 There may have been other reasons라고 하면 된다. 비슷한 의미로 That's one possible reason(이것은 어디까지나 하나의 가능성입니다)이라고도 말할 수 있다.

Note In the last example, the presenter uses the sentence, **There may have been other reasons**. A similar sentence is **That's one possible reason**.

10.8 Speculating on the reason for something using probably, because of, one possible reason is, one possible explanation is, perhaps 원인을 추측한다: 확신 정도를 낮추기 위한 표현

Here the presenter gives possible reasons for something, but uses less direct language such as **probably**, **because of**, **one possible reason is**, **one possible explanation is** and **perhaps**.

추측하는 원인을 말할 때, 필요에 따라 확신하는 정도를 낮추는 표현(probably 등)으로 청중에게 '확실히 알 수는 없다'는 점을 강조할 수 있다.

~ 의 원인은 아마 ~이지 않을까 싶습니다.

- The reason for the sudden increase in temperature was probably the increased reaction time.

Probably 아마

- The reason for the sudden increase in temperature was probably the increased reaction time.
- The sudden increase in temperature was probably because of the addition of another catalyst.
- The sudden increase in temperature was probably as a result of the reduction in the number of samples.
- The sudden increase in temperature was probably due to the reduction in the number of samples.

Because of ~의 원인에 의해

- We don't know the reason for this. It might be because of the number of samples. Another reason might be the size of the samples.

One possible reason is 생각할 수 있는 원인 중 하나는 ~

- We don't know why the samples cracked. One possible reason is the higher temperature.

● One possible explanation is 생각할 수 있는 설명 중 하나는 ~

- We aren't sure why the experiment failed. One possible explanation is a buildup of pressure in the system.
- We aren't sure why the experiment failed. One possible explanation is an increase of pressure in the system.

● Perhaps 어쩌면

- Perhaps something happened in the central nervous system. We really don't know at the moment. We are still working on that.

In this example, there are three steps. First, the presenter offers a possible reason for something. Perhaps something happened in the central nervous system. Next, it is stated that the reason is unknown. We really don't know at the moment. Finally, it is stated that further research work is being conducted on this issue. We are still working on that.

왼쪽의 예문은 '어쩌면 ~ 일지도 모르겠습니다' → '그러나 현시점에서는 아직 잘 모르고 있습니다' → '이 점에 대해서는 현재도 연구를 진행하고 있습니다'의 3단계로 설명하고 있다.

10.9 When you cannot explain something, refer to future work
설명하기 어려운 상황의 대응(1): 향후 연구에 관해 언급한다

When they cannot explain why something happens, some presenters refer to future work.

~의 원인은 모르겠습니다. 이 점에 대해서는 앞으로 연구를 계속 진행할 예정입니다.

- We are not sure why this happens. We are planning to do further experiments on this issue.
- We are not sure of the cause of the problem. We are carrying out more experiments on this issue.
- We don't know the reason for this issue. We are still working on it.

현시점의 데이터로는 설명이 어려운 내용에 대해서는 '~에 관해서는 현재 조사 중입니다 / 향후 연구를 예정하고 있습니다'와 같이 말할 수도 있다.

10.10 Using the word basically to explain something simply
설명하기 어려운 상황의 대응(2): 단순화하여 설명한다

The word basically is a useful way of giving a short, simple explanation.

~에 대해 설명하는 것은 어렵지만, 간단히 말하면 ~입니다.

- **I'm not sure how to describe it. Basically, it is a 2-step reaction with the addition of a catalyst.**
- **I'm not sure how to explain it. Basically, it is a 2-step reaction with the addition of a catalyst.**
- **It's difficult to explain. Basically, it is a 2 step-reaction with addition of a catalyst.**

정확하게 설명하기 어려운 경우에는 basically(간단히 말하면/기본적으로는)를 문장 앞에 두고 단순/간략하게 설명한다.

11 Introducing references

참고문헌을 제시하는 방법 / 결과를 선행 연구와 비교하는 방법

Here I give examples of how to introduce references and URLs.

11.1 Referring to references on your slides with the following words and expressions: here, check, check out, look at, take a look at, describe, description, find, see 참고문헌을 제시한다

I have noticed that more presenters are including references on their slides. Here, I give examples of how to introduce them. Please remember to use the pointer to draw the attention of the audience to the reference / references.

구두발표 슬라이드에 참고문헌을 제시하여 자세한 내용은 이를 참고해 달라고 말한다.

Script(자세한 설명은 생략하고, 참고문헌을 활용해 달라고 요청하는 예시)

This slide shows the experimental setup. I'll skip the exact details of the apparatus. If you are interested, here are the references, which give a detailed explanation of the apparatus.

관심 있는 분께서는 여기의 참고문헌을 활용해 주시기 바랍니다.

- If you are interested, here are the references, which give a detailed explanation of the apparatus.

● Here

- Here are the references.
- Here are the relevant references.

Here라는 용어를 사용할 때는 슬라이드의 참고문헌 목록을 레이저 포인터로 가리키면서 '이것이 참고문헌입니다'라고 말한다.

● Check

- Please check this reference / these references.
- If you want to see the details, please check this reference / these references.

Check ~, check out ~, look at ~, take a look at ~ 등의 용어를 사용하는 경우는 '여기의 참고문헌을 확인해 주세요'라고 말한다.

- Check out

- If you are interested in the details, please check out this reference / these references.

- Look at

- If you want to see the details, please look at this reference / these references.

- Take a look at

- If you are interested in the details, please take a look at this reference / these references.

- Describe

- The system / setup / approach is described in detail in this reference.
- The system / setup / approach is described here.

Describe(동사) 또는 description(명사) 등의 용어를 사용하는 경우는 '~에 대해서는 이 참고문헌에 잘 언급되어 있습니다', '이 문헌에는 ~에 대해 자세히 나와 있습니다'라고 표현한다.

- Description

- This reference contains a detailed description of the experimental set up.
- There is a description of the method in this reference.

- Find

- You can find a detailed explanation of this process here.

Find 또는 see 등의 단어를 사용할 때는 '~에 대한 자세한 내용은 여기 참고문헌에서 찾아보실 수 있습니다'라고 표현한다.

- See

- You can see the details in this reference / these references.
- You can see our other work here.
- You can see our other work in these references.
- You can see that approach in these references.

11.2 How to refer to URLs
참고할 수 있는 URL을 제시한다

In addition to referring to references, you might want to draw people's attention to URLs that contain relevant information.

Script(참고할 수 있는 URL에 대해 설명하는 예시)

So these are the main areas of research that we cover at our institute. A more detailed explanation can be found in this URL.

여기의 URL을 참고해 주십시오.

- I've included some relevant URLs here.
- Here are some useful URLs.
- You might find these URLs useful.
- If you are interested, please check these URLs.

웹사이트의 URL을 소개할 때는 왼쪽과 같이 말한다.

11.3 How to use the expression in the literature
결과를 선행 연구와 비교한다: in the literature 표현의 사용법

It is important to put your data in the context of results in the same field. For that reason, presenters compare their findings to what has been reported elsewhere. The phrase **in the literature** is frequently used. Here are some examples.

Script(발표자의 실험 결과와 선행 연구에서 보고된 내용을 서로 비교하는 예시)

So, as you can see from the results, we obtained a yield of 5 to 6 percent. Similar yields are reported in the literature.

선행 연구/문헌에서는 ~라고 보고하고 있습니다.

- **Similar yields are reported in the literature.**

Examples

- **In the literature, reported values** are in the region of 5 to 6 percent.
- **Reported values in the literature** are in the region of 5 to 6 percent.
- **This means that our results are in line with the literature.**

Common errors — 흔히 하는 실수

✕ *In literature,* values are in the region of 5 to 6 percent.

✕ *In literatures,* values are in the region of 5 to 6 percent.

○ **In the literature,** values are in the region of 5 to 6 percent.

○ **In the literature,** average values were in the region of 5 to 6 percent.

Literature는 집합명사이어서 단어 앞에 정관사 **the**를 붙여야 하고, 불가산명사이기도 하므로 단어 뒤에 **s**는 붙이지 않는다. 따라서 문헌의 수와 관계없이 항상 **in the literature**의 형태로 표현해야 한다.

In literature, should be **in the literature**. The word literature is classified as a group or collective noun, and therefore needs a definite article. *In literatures* is incorrect. Literature is not countable and is a collective noun. Generally, the word literature is not plural

✕ *In their literature,* Watanabe reported values are in the region of 5 to 6 percent.

○ **Watanabe 2018 reported** values in the region of 5 to 6 percent.

특정 논문을 가리켜 'ㅇㅇ 등의 논문'이라고 말할 때 *in their literature*라고 하면 잘못된 표현이다. 왼쪽과 같이 '저자명+발표년'의 형태로 표현한다.

This is a reference relating to a specific paper. It is not possible to say *in their literature*. It is better to state the **author** and **year of the paper** in this pattern, **Watanabe 2018 reported**.

✕ Based on *many literature*, we decided to use a value of 15 percent.

◯ Based on the literature, we decided to use a value of 15 percent

The expression *many literature* is incorrect because literature is a collective noun and is generally singular.

Literature는 집합명사이므로 '많다', '적다' 등의 수량으로 표현할 수 없다.

11.4 Other expressions using the word literature
문헌에 관한 그 외의 표현

Here are some more examples that use the word **literature**.

이 결과는 선행 연구에서 보고된 결과와 일치합니다

- This means that our results are in line with reported values in the literature.
- This means that our results are in line with the literature.
- This means that our results are much the same as those reported in the literature.
- These results are pretty similar to what is in the literature.
- This result is consistent with what is in the literature.

발표자의 연구 결과가 선행 연구의 결과와 일치한다고 언급할 때는 왼쪽처럼 in line with ~, much the same as ~, pretty similar to ~, consistent with ~ 등의 표현을 활용한다.

관련 문헌에 따르면 ~입니다.

- Based on a literature review, we found average yields were in the region of 2 million tons.
- Based on a review of the literature, we found average yields were in the region of 2 million tons.

12 Summarizing at 3 levels: one slide, several slides, a section
발표 중간에 요약을 끼워 넣는 방법: 슬라이드 한 장의 요약, 슬라이드 여러 장의 요약, 일정 부분의 요약

This section contains sentences that will help you to summarize information at 3 different levels as follows: **one slide**, **several slides**, and **a section**.

Many presenters think that there is only one summary in a presentation, and that it is always at the end of the presentation. In fact, during a presentation, you will probably want to **give several mini-summaries**, **in addition to** a summary at the end of the presentation. These mini-summaries can be at the level of **one slide**, **several slides** or **a section**.

대개의 발표자는 발표가 거의 끝나는 마지막 부분에서만 요약을 언급하지만, 발표 중간중간에 앞선 내용을 요약해가면 청중들의 이해를 돕는 데 효과적이다.

이번 항목에서는 (1) 슬라이드 한 장의 내용을 요약하는 방법, (2) 슬라이드 몇 장의 내용을 요약하는 방법, (3) 일정 부분의 내용을 요약하는 방법 등의 3단계 요약 방법을 소개한다.

12.1 Summarizing one slide
앞선 내용을 요약한다(1): 슬라이드 한 장의 요약

It is not necessary to summarize the information presented in every slide, but if a slide has a lot of data or is particularly important, it will help the audience if you can briefly stress the main points in the form of a short summary. In some cases, the main point or points will be presented at the bottom of the slide. In the example below, the expression, **the substrate is thinner and more flexible**, can be positioned at the bottom of the slide.

정보가 많거나 중요한 슬라이드에서 발표자가 핵심적인 내용을 요약해 주면 청중이 이해하는 데 큰 도움을 줄 수 있다. 특히 말로 요약하는 것 외에 슬라이드의 맨 아래에 요약한 문장을 짧게 넣는 것도 좋은 방법이다.

In most cases, summarizing a single slide will be in the form of a main point or points, or some kind of take-home message. Here are some examples.

다음 쪽 예시의 경우, 슬라이드 맨 아래에 **the substrate is thinner and more flexible**이라는 요약문을 넣었다. 슬라이드 아래에 요약문을 만드는 방법은 96~98쪽을 참고한다.

이 슬라이드의 핵심은 ~입니다.

- The key point/issue here is that the substrate is thinner and more flexible.
- The thing to remember here is that the substrate is thinner and more flexible.
- So, the main point in this slide is that the substrate is thinner and more flexible.
- The main message here is that the substrate is thinner and more flexible.
- The take-home message from this data is that the substrate is thinner and more flexible.

마지막 예문에서 사용한 take-home message(청중이 집으로 꼭 가져가야 할 중요 메시지)라는 표현은 발표 전체의 요약뿐 아니라, 슬라이드 한 장이나 몇 장을 요약할 때도 활용할 수 있다.

Note The expression the take-home message is can be used to summarize data in a single slide, a section, as well as in a summary slide at the end of the presentation.

12.2 Summarizing several slides
앞선 내용을 요약한다(2): 슬라이드 여러 장의 요약

To summarize the main points from several slides, presenters use a 2-step system as follows: **1. Signal the start of the summary 2. Briefly list the main points**. Here are some examples.

앞선 슬라이드 여러 장의 내용을 요약할 때는 ① 이제 내용을 요약하겠다는 언급을 한 후 → ② 요점을 몇 가지로 정리하는 두 단계로 진행한다.

여기서 잠시 좀 전에 말씀드린 몇 장의 슬라이드 내용을 요약해 보겠습니다. 핵심은 ~입니다.

- We have covered quite a lot of ground. So I'd like to summarize what we have seen in the last few slides. (short summary of the main points)
- I'd like to summarize what we have seen in the last few slides. The main points are (short summary of the main points)
- This is what we have seen in the last few slides. (short summary of the main points)

'좀 전에 말씀드린 몇 장의 슬라이드'는 last few slides로 표현한다.

12.3 Summarizing a section
앞선 내용을 요약한다(3): 일정 부분의 요약

이 부분을 요약하겠습니다. 핵심은 ~입니다.

- **I'd like to wrap up this section by summarizing the main points.** (short summary of the main points)
- **I'd just like to summarize the main points in this section.** (short summary of the main points)
- **I'll just go over the main points in this section.** (short summary of the main points)
- **I'll just run through the main points from this section.** (short summary of the main points)
- **The take-home message for this section is as follows.** (short summary of the main points)
- **These are the main points from this section.** (short summary of the main points)

요약한다는 뜻을 표현할 때 **wrap up ~, go over ~, run through ~** 등의 구동사를 사용하면 편리하다. 이런 구동사에 대해서는 Part 5의 188~190쪽을 참고한다.

13 From data to explanation and implications
결과를 고찰하는 방법: 결과가 무엇을 의미하는지 / 어떤 의의가 있는지

A lot of time will be spent introducing data and results. For the audience to be able to process what is presented, the presenter will need to explain the meaning of the data, and the implications.

Here is an example.

연구 결과를 설명할 때는 단순히 어떤 결과를 얻었다는 언급뿐 아니라 그 결과가 무엇을 의미하는지, 학술적으로나 실용적으로 어떤 의의가 있는지 등에 대해서도 함께 고찰해야 한다.

Script(어떤 결과인지 → 무엇을 의미하는지 → 어떤 의의가 있는지 등의 순서로 설명하는 예시)

The data shows an increase in temperature and reaction speed. This means that molecules are excited and move freely. In terms of manufacturing, we can fabricate thinner, more flexible films.

13.1 Introduce the data on the slide
어떤 결과를 얻었는지 소개한다

The following examples are simple statements of what is on the slide.

이 결과로부터 ~라는 것을 알 수 있습니다.

- The data shows an increase in temperature and reaction speed.
- As you can see from the data I have presented, there is an increase in temperature and reaction speed.
- What we have seen from this data is that there is an increase in temperature and reaction speed.

결과를 나타내는 도표에서 무엇(예: 수치의 상승)을 알 수 있는지 설명할 때 왼쪽과 같은 표현을 활용한다.

13.2 Explain the data
결과가 무엇을 의미하는지 설명한다

Here the presenter gives an explanation of the data presented using the expressions, This means that, This suggests that, So these results tell us that.

이 결과는 ~라는 것을 의미하고 있습니다.

- This means that molecules are excited and move freely.
- This suggests that molecules are excited and move freely.
- So, these results tell us that molecules are excited and move freely.

13.1에서 설명한 결과가 무엇을 의미하는지 설명할 때는 This means that ~, This suggests that ~, So ~, these results tell us that ~ 등의 표현을 활용한다.

13.3 Explain the implications
결과가 갖는 의의를 설명한다

At this point. the presenter comments on how the data affects the wider picture, which in this case is the manufacturing process.

○○ 분야에서, 이 결과가 갖는 의의는/미치는 영향은 ~입니다.

- In terms of manufacturing, we can fabricate thinner more flexible films.
- The main implications for the manufacturing process are that thinner and more flexible films can be obtained.
- So, what this means is that we are able to manufacture more flexible films.
- So, the important point here is that we can manufacture thinner and more flexible films.

The presenter brings in the wider picture using the expressions in terms of and the main implications are to introduce the point.

이 연구의 결과가 다른 연구에 어떤 영향을 미치는지, 어떤 실용적 의의가 있는지 등을 설명할 때는 왼쪽과 같이 표현한다.

In terms of ○○를 사용하여 '○○ 분야에서 ~'라고 명확하게 표현하는 것이 좋다.

14 Introducing and explaining a video clip
동영상을 재생하고 설명하는 방법

The number of presenters using short video clips in their presentations has increased, but simply showing a video clip is not enough. The presenter needs to support the video clip with appropriate English. Below I have listed several useful sentences.

구두발표에서 동영상을 활용하면 효과가 크다. 하지만 동영상을 단순히 보여 주는 것만으로는 충분하지 않으므로 중요한 부분을 말로써 보충하여 설명해야 한다.

14.1 Introducing a video clip
재생할 동영상을 소개한다

지금부터 ~의 동영상을 보여 드리겠습니다.

- I'm going to show you a short video of the catalytic conversion.
- I'd like to show you a video clip of the reaction.
- I'm going to show you a video clip of the reaction.
- I have a video clip of the reaction that I'm going to show you.
- This is a video clip of the reaction.

처음에 무엇에 관련된 동영상인지 한 문장으로 간략히 설명한다.

Common errors — 흔히 하는 실수

✕ Please *look at* the video.
✕ Please *watch* this video.
○ I'm going to show you a video clip of the reaction.
○ This is a video clip of the reaction.

The expressions *please look at* and *please watch* are incorrect. Better expressions are as follows: **I'd like to show you a video clip. I'm going to show you a video clip. This is a video clip of the reaction.**

동영상을 재생할 때 *please look at* 또는 *please watch* 등의 표현을 쓰면 안 된다. 이 경우에 I'd like to show you a video clip 등으로 말하는 것이 좋다.

14.2 Describing a number of stages in a process or reaction
동영상의 각 단계를 설명한다

Script(동영상의 각 단계에 대한 설명 → 동영상의 요약 등의 순서로 설명하는 예시)

① At this point, the sample is stable and there is no reaction. ② Here you can see the first stages of the reaction. The edge of the sample is changing color. ③ This is followed by combustion. ④ Finally, the sample becomes hard. ⑤ So, what is the significance of the chemical reaction? I think we have seen that the reaction is stable. ⑥ This means that the process has various possible applications.

Key sentences

1. Start the explanation 어떤 현상이 일어나기 전의 상태에 관해 설명한다.

이 시점에서는 ~입니다.

- **At this point, the sample is stable and there is no reaction.**

Examples

- **At this stage**, the sample is stable and there is no reaction.
- **Here**, the sample is stable and there is no reaction.
- **So, in the beginning**, the sample is stable and there is no reaction.

학회 발표에서 동영상을 활용할 때는 어떤 현상(예: 화학 반응)의 전체 과정을 생생하게 보여 주기 위한 경우가 많으므로, 그 현상의 단계마다 말로써 설명해 주는 것이 좋다.

첫 번째로, 동영상 재생을 시작하는 시점(어떤 현상이 시작되기 전)의 상태를 설명한다. '이 시점에서는'은 At this point 등으로 표현한다.

2. Move on to the next stage 처음 일어나는 변화를 설명한다

보시는 것처럼 ~가 시작되었습니다.

- Here you can see the first stages of the reaction.

Examples

- As you can see, these are the first stages of the reaction.
- Here we can observe the initial stages of the reaction quite clearly.
- So, this is the start of the first stages of the reaction.

어떤 현상이 시작되었음을 표현할 때는 왼쪽과 같이 말한다. '보시는 것처럼, (지금 현상이 시작되었습니다)'는 Here you can see ~ 또는 As you can see ~ 등으로 말한다.

3. Introduce the following stage 다음 상태를 설명한다

이어서, ~이 일어납니다.

- This is followed by combustion.

Examples

- And next, the sample catches on fire.
- After that, we get combustion.
- At this point, combustion takes place.
- And now, combustion takes place.

다음에 일어나는 변화에 대해서는 왼쪽처럼 설명한다. A is followed by B는 'A에 이어서 B가 일어난다'라는 표현이다.

4. Explain the last stage 최종 상태를 설명한다

마지막에는 ~이 됩니다.

- Finally, the sample becomes hard.

Examples

- This is the last stage of the reaction. And the sample becomes hard.
- The sample is hard.
- The sample becomes hard.
- In the end, the sample becomes hard.
- By the time the reaction finishes, the sample becomes hard.

동영상의 최종 상태(어떤 현상이 모두 종료)를 설명하고 동영상의 재생을 끝낸다.

14.3 Signal the start of the explanation
동영상의 중요한 내용을 설명한다

이 동영상의 요점은 무엇일까요?

- So, what is the significance of the chemical reaction?

Examples

- We have seen various stages of the reaction. The question is, what is the significance of it?

동영상을 재생한 후에는 어떤 점이 중요한지 강조하고 동영상의 내용을 요약한다. 설명을 시작할 때 왼쪽처럼 말한다.

14.4 Concluding the video sequence with an explanation
요점을 말하고 동영상에 대한 설명을 마친다

이 동영상의 요점은 ~입니다. 이것은 ~을 의미합니다.

- I think we have seen that the reaction is stable. This means that the process has various possible applications.

Examples

- What we have seen is that the reaction has 4 stages.
- So, this shows that the reaction is stable, and can be applied to various industrial processes.
- I think we have seen the reaction is stable. This means it can be controlled.
- This means that the process can be used industrially for a variety of uses.

동영상에서 무엇이 중요하고 그것이 어떤 의미인지 설명한다.

15 Time management, correcting yourself, correcting an error on a slide
발표 시간의 관리 / 발언 또는 슬라이드 내용의 정정

Here I include some useful expressions concerning time issues, how to correct yourself and dealing with an error on the slide.

15.1 Time management
발표 시간의 관리

If you think you don't have enough time left, you can use these sentences.

시간이 부족해서 ~로 바로 넘어가겠습니다 / ~는 생략합니다.

- I'm running out of time. So, I'll move on to the discussion section.
- Since time is short, I'll go straight to the summary.
- I don't have much time left, so I'll skip these slides.

발표 시간이 부족하여 일부 내용을 건너뛸 때는 왼쪽과 같이 말한다. 슬라이드를 건너뛸 때 활용하는 표현은 132쪽을 참고한다.

If you spoke over the time limit, you can use this sentence.

발표 시간을 1~2분 초과해 버렸습니다. 미안합니다.

- Sorry. I think I went over by a minute or two.

발표 시간을 넘긴 경우, 왼쪽 표현으로 청중에게 사과하는 뜻을 전한다 '(시간을) 초과하다'는 go over (by + 시간)라는 표현을 사용한다.

15.2 Correcting yourself
발언 내용을 바로잡는다

In some cases, you will need to correct what you have just said. For example, you might have misread a number or said something incorrectly.

말로 한 설명이 잘못된 경우는 왼쪽과 같이 바로잡는다. 사과 → 정정의 순서로 하는데 사과는 **Excuse me** 또는 **I'm sorry**, 정정은 **I meant to say / should have said** (+ 올바른 내용) **not** (+ 잘못된 내용) 등으로 말한다.

실례했습니다. ××가 아니라 ○○입니다.

- Excuse me, I meant to say 150 not 250.
- I'm sorry. I should have said that temperature increased not decreased.

15.3 Correcting an error on a slide
슬라이드의 내용을 바로잡는다

죄송합니다. 슬라이드에 오류가 있었습니다. ××가 아니라 ○○입니다.

- I've just seen a mistake on this slide. The title should be degradable not non-degradable.
- Excuse me, that number should be 179 not 197.
- I'm sorry. That should be 179.
- Excuse me. That should read 179.
- Sorry that's a mistake. It should be 179 not 197.

슬라이드의 내용에 오류가 있었다면 왼쪽과 같이 **that should be** (+ 올바른 내용) **not** (+ 잘못된 내용)의 표현으로 바로잡는다.

16 How to use the expressions stand for and is short for to introduce an acronym

두문자어(acronym)를 설명하는 방법

In the example below, the acronym is AIST and the full title is introduced with the 2-word verb **stands for**. Another expression that you can use is, **is short for**

Acronym은 '두문자어'라고 하며, 여러 단어의 머리 글자를 연결하여 하나의 단어로 만든 줄임말이다.

ㅇㅇ(두문자어)는 ~의 약자입니다.

- AIST **stands for** Advanced Institute of Science and Technology.
- AIST **is short for** Advanced Institute of Science and Technology.

Acronym을 설명할 때는 stands for ~ 또는 is short for ~ 중에 하나를 사용한다. 이 경우에 mean은 사용할 수 없으니 주의한다.

Common errors — 흔히 하는 실수

✕ AIST, ***in short***, Advanced Institute of Science and Technology.

✕ AIST, ***shortly***, Advanced Institute of Science and Technology.

✕ AIST, ***short for***, Advanced Institute of Science and Technology.

✕ AIST, ***means***, Advanced Institute of Science and Technology.

○ AIST **stands for** Advanced Institute of Science and Technology.

○ AIST **is short for** Advanced Institute of Science and Technology.

The above errors should be changed to **stands for** or **is short for**. These expressions have the same meaning. Please note that the word ***means*** cannot be used to introduce an acronym.

17 Giving examples using such as, for example, for instance
구체적인 예를 들어 설명하는 방법

Script(for example이라는 표현에 이어서, 구체적인 장점을 열거하는 예시)

Although amalgam has traces of mercury, it does have several advantages, for example hardness, durability and cost.

I'm surprised that presenters fail to give examples, especially when a simple example would help the audience to understand the point being made. Here I introduce three of the most frequently used expressions for introducing examples.

발표자는 청중이 이해하기 쉽도록 구체적인 예를 들어 설명하는 것이 좋다. 구체적인 예를 말로 전달할 때는 **such as**, **for example**, **for instance** 등의 표현을 활용한다.

예를 들면 ○○(구체적인 예)입니다. / ○○(구체적인 예) 등의 ~.

- The samples should be treated with some kind of nucleophile, **such as** alcohol or ether.
- The system is susceptible to factors **such as** moisture, temperature and vibration.
- This was calculated using variables **such as** speed, weight and mass.
- I'll just quickly mention some possible applications. The system can be used in various ways, **such as / for example / for instance**, medical applications.

17.1 How to introduce an example. Referring to material on the slide you are currently showing
슬라이드에 구체적인 예를 표시한다(1): 현재의 슬라이드

Here I show how to introduce examples with the expressions: This is, Here we have, Here are, I'll show you, I'll give you.

이런 예가 있습니다.

- This is an example.
- This is an example of the reaction process.
- This is a typical example.
- Here we have a typical example.
- Here are some examples.

구체적인 예를 들 때는 말 외에도 슬라이드에 직접 표시하여 설명할 수도 있다. 현재의 슬라이드에 구체적인 예가 제시된 경우에는 왼쪽과 같이 표현하는 것이 좋다.

17.2 How to introduce an example when referring to material on the next slide
슬라이드에 구체적인 예를 표시한다(2): 다음 슬라이드

구체적인 예는 다음 슬라이드에서 보여 드리겠습니다.

- I'll show you an example in the next slide / later.
- I'll show you some examples in the next slide.
- I'll give you some examples of that in the next slide.
- I'll introduce some examples of the system in the next section.

다음 슬라이드에서 구체적인 예를 보여 주겠다고 예고할 때는 왼쪽과 같이 말한다.

18 Explaining a process using the words first, next, after that, then
순서를 설명하는 방법

In this example, the presenter uses **first**, **next**, **after that**, and **then** to explain a process. This is a standard way of sequencing a number of steps.

먼저 ~을 했습니다. 다음으로 ~하고, 마지막으로 ~했습니다.

- **First,** the samples were washed. **Next,** they were dried. **After that** they were stored. **Then** we calculated the difference in weight.

실험 절차 등을 설명할 때는 first, next, after that, then 등의 순서를 나타내는 표현을 활용한다.

It is also possible to reduce the length of the sentence by deleting the words **first**, **next**, **after that**, and **then**.

- **We washed, dried and stored the samples. Then, we calculated the difference in weight.**

왼쪽처럼, 순서를 나타내는 단어를 생략하여 더 간결하게 말할 수도 있다.

Column #04

Is it okay to read from the text on your computer?

구두발표를 할 때 미리 작성한 원고를 그대로 읽어도 괜찮을까?

Nowadays, computers are equipped with a handy tool that means you can write the script for your presentation at the bottom of the screen and read from it. Some presenters ask me if this okay. Personally, I do not think this is a problem. As you are speaking, the audience will be busy looking at the slides and listening to your explanation, and no one will notice that you are reading from a script. There is, however, one problem. Because you are reading from the computer screen, your presentation may appear to be flat and rather monotonous. You can avoid this problem if you have a script that is informal and uses spoken English, not formal, written English. Of course, it would be better if you could give a presentation without a script, but for many presenters this is too difficult. Reading from the script is acceptable and is one step on the way to giving a presentation without notes.

미리 작성한 원고를 읽으면 발표가 딱딱하고 단조로워지기 쉽다. 원고를 보지 않고 발표하는 것이 좋지만, 그렇지 못하다면 구어체의 영어를 활용함으로써 이런 문제를 줄일 수 있다.

Part 5

Finishing your presentation
발표를 끝내는 방법

In this part of the book, I introduce a 16-step guide for finishing your presentation. The focus is on useful sentences and vocabulary that will help you to give a clear and concise summary of the main points of your presentation.

발표의 마지막에는 발표 내용의 요점을 간략하게 정리한 후에 청중에게 감사 인사를 하고 발표를 모두 끝낸다. 이번 장에서는 발표를 마무리하는 흐름을 16단계로 나누어 소개하며, 이때 사용하는 '요약 슬라이드'에 대해서는 다음(Part 6)에 해설하기로 한다.

Presentation styles have changed. Previously, presenters signaled the end of their presentation with, In conclusion, and used formal written language such as, It was suggested that or Within the limitations of this study, we could achieve significant improvements in performance. Slides consisted of full sentences, which the presenter read out word for word. In some cases, the presenter said nothing and expected the audience to read what was on the last slide. The last part of the presentation was flat and had little or no impact.

Today, presenters finish their presentations with sentences such as: This is my last slide, This is a summary, This is the take-home message. The final slide consists of a short summary of the main points of the presentation, presented on the slide with bullet points. These are supported by a script using simple English. The English on the slide and the script are different. It is common to mention future research, funding and acknowledgments. The summary slide has become more complex, includes more information, and is a crucial part of the presentation.

• 이전의 학회 발표에서는 일반적으로, 마지막 슬라이드에 논문 문장처럼 작성한 결론을 발표자가 읽는 것으로 발표의 끝을 맺었다.

• 하지만 최근에는 발표 내용의 요점을 조목조목 정리한 슬라이드를 만들고, 그것을 간결한 영어로 정리하는 방식을 많이 활용한다.

Finishing: A 16-step guide for finishing your presentation
발표를 마무리하는 16단계

Starting the summary: Steps 1~5
요약을 시작한다: 1~5단계

1. Signal the start of the summary 〈최종적으로 요약하겠다는 의사 표현을 한다〉
2. Remind the audience of your current research 〈현재의 연구 내용을 다시 한번 말한다〉
3. Remind the audience of the topic 〈발표 주제를 다시 한번 말한다〉
4. Restate the objectives 〈연구 목적을 다시 한번 말한다〉
5. Restate research questions 〈의문 · 가설을 다시 한번 말한다〉

Introduce the findings, additional findings, the main message, the take-home message, implications, and future work: Steps 6~11
연구 결과의 요점이나 청중에게 보내는 메시지를 말한다: 6~11단계

6. Introduce the findings 〈결과를 소개한다〉
   - 6.1 Signal the start of the findings
   - 6.2 Stating the findings
   - 6.3 Introducing additional findings
7. Explain the findings 〈결과로부터 얻을 수 있는 결론을 설명한다〉
   - 7.1 Introduce the start of the explanation
   - 7.2 Main message
8. State the take-home message 〈청중에게 가장 전하고 싶은 핵심적인 메시지를 말한다〉
9. Mention the implications 〈연구의 의의를 말한다〉
10. Finishing 〈요약을 끝낸다〉
11. Mention future work 〈이후의 연구 과제를 말한다〉

Finishing the presentation: Steps 12~16
발표를 마친다: 12~16단계

12. Funding 〈연구비 지원에 관하여 언급한다〉
13. Acknowledgments 〈감사의 마음을 전한다〉
14. Signal the end of the presentation 〈마무리 인사를 한다〉
15. Contact details 〈발표자의 연락처를 알려준다〉
16. Invite questions 〈질문을 받는다〉

1 Starting the summary: Steps 1-5
요약을 시작한다: 1~5단계

1 Signal the start of the summary
최종적으로 요약하겠다는 의사 표현을 한다

Here are some examples of how to signal the start of the summary using the words **last**, **finish**, **summary**, **summarize**, **run through**, **go over**, **wrap up**.

이제, 지금까지의 발표 내용을 최종적으로 요약하겠다는 의사 표현을 하나의 문장으로 말한다. 이때 last, finish, summary, summarize, run through, go over, wrap up 등의 용어 중에서 하나를 활용한다(이 가운데 하나만으로 충분하며, 여러 표현을 조합하지 않아도 된다).

● Last

이것이 마지막 슬라이드입니다.

- This is the last slide.
- This is my last slide.

Note Both of the following expressions are possible: the last slide and my last slide.

Last를 사용하는 경우는 '이것이 마지막 슬라이드(=요약 슬라이드)입니다'와 같이 말한다. '마지막 슬라이드'는 the last slide 또는 my last slide로 표현한다(일반적으로 학회 발표에서는 my라는 용어를 피해야 하지만 이 상황에서는 사용할 수 있다. 자세한 것은 16쪽 칼럼을 참고한다).

● Finish

마지막으로 요약을 하고, 오늘의 발표를 모두 마치도록 하겠습니다

- I'd like to finish with a summary.
- I'm going to finish by making the following points.
- I want to finish by summarizing the main points / the main findings.
- I want to finish by going over the main points.
- I'm going to finish by reviewing the main points.

Note Frequently used patterns are as follows: finish with a summary, finish by verb+ing, summarizing, reviewing, talking about, + the main points, the main findings.

Finish를 이용하는 경우는 finish with a summary 또는 finish by ~ing the main points/findings 중에 하나로 표현한다.

Summary

이것이 오늘 발표의 요약입니다.

- This is a summary.
- I'd like to finish with a summary.
- This is a summary of the main points I made today.
- This is a summary of the main points.
- This is a summary of the main findings.
- This is a summary of the results.

'요약을 말씀드리겠다'라고 할 때는 명사 summary와 동사 summarize를 모두 사용할 수 있다.

Summarize

오늘의 발표 내용을 요약하겠습니다.

- I'd like to summarize my presentation.
- I'd like to summarize the findings.
- I'd like to summarize the main points I made today.
- I'm going to summarize this presentation.
- I want to summarize the main points.
- I'll (quickly) summarize the main points / the most important findings.

Run through

오늘 발표의 요점을 정리하겠습니다.

- I'd like to run through the main points I made today.
- I'm going to run through the main points.
- I'll (just) run through the main points.

Run through ~는 '요점만을 간단히 설명한다'는 뜻의 구동사이다. 세 번째 예문의 just 역시 '요점만을 간단히'라는 뜻으로, 이는 생략할 수 있다.

Note The word **just** signals that the presenter will **briefly explain the main points**. It is possible to omit **just** as the two-word verb **run through** indicates that what follows is a short summary of the main points.

Go over

오늘 발표의 요점을 되돌아보겠습니다.

- I'd like to go over the main points.
- I want to go over the main findings.
- I'd like to go over the main points I covered today.
- I'm going to go over the main findings (in this work / study / research).

Go over ~도 run through ~와 같은 어감의 용어이다. 많은 정보 중에서 중요한 내용만을 요약해서 설명할 때 편리한 표현이다.

Note The verbs run through and go over mean to explain something briefly, and are particularly useful when you have a lot of information but can only focus on the main points.

Wrap up

오늘 발표를 요약하고자 합니다.

- I'm going to wrap up this presentation.
- I'd like to wrap up this presentation with a short summary.
- I want to wrap up this presentation by talking about the main results and mentioning our future work.
- I want to wrap up this presentation by going over the main points and talking about future directions.
- I'm going to wrap up this presentation by reviewing the main points and talking about future directions.

Wrap up ~은 '요약하다', '마무리하다', '끝내다' 등의 뜻을 가진 구동사로, 발표를 마칠 때 자주 사용한다.

Note Any of the examples in this section, 1. Signal the start of the summary, can be used alone to start the summary. It is not necessary to combine them. Just one sentence from this section is enough to signal that you will start the summary.

여기까지 소개된 예문 중에서 하나를 활용하면 충분하므로 여러 표현을 조합하지 않아도 된다.

2 Remind the audience of your current research interests
현재의 연구 내용을 다시 한번 말한다

Some presenters **briefly refer to their current research interests.** In most cases, this is just a single sentence.

어떤 발표자들은 요약 첫 부분에서 자신이 어떤 연구를 하고 있는지 간단히 언급하기도 한다.

저희는 ~에 대한 연구를 하고 있습니다.

- **We have been working on** ways of reducing energy loss in this device.
- **We have been developing** a number of experimental methods for schizophrenia.
- **Over a number of years, we have been investigating** ways of reducing energy loss in this device.
- **We have been studying** ways of reducing energy loss.
- **We have been looking at** ways of reducing energy loss.

연구 내용을 설명할 때는 현재완료진행형(**have been ~ing**)으로 표현한다. 이는 자신의 연구가 과거에 시작되어 현재도 계속 진행 중임을 나타낸다.

Note The easiest way of reminding the audience of your current research is with the phrase **We have been working on + research topic.** The pattern is **We have been working on + (topic).** This pattern refers to work that started some time ago and is ongoing. Another useful sentence is, **We have been looking at + research topic.**

3 Remind the audience of the presentation topic
발표 주제를 다시 한번 말한다

It is common for presenters to **state the topic of the presentation again.** This is just **to remind the audience of the topic** and **to focus on what was studied.** Although this is just a short sentence, it is a very effective way of starting the summary.

발표 주제를 다시 언급하면 청중들이 발표 내용을 되새기기 쉽다.

오늘은 ~에 대해서 말씀드렸습니다.

- Today, I talked about water pollution in agricultural areas.
- We looked at water pollution in agricultural areas.
- So, we looked at water pollution in agricultural areas.
- Today, I focused on water pollution in agricultural areas.

Note Probably, the easiest way of reminding the audience of the presentation topic is with the patterns We looked at + topic and So, we looked at + topic.

발표 주제를 말할 때는 (So,) we looked at + topic으로 말하는 것이 가장 간단한 표현이다.

4 Restate the objectives
연구 목적을 다시 한번 말한다

Briefly restating the objectives of the study will help the audience.

이 연구는 ~을 밝히기 위한 목적으로 시행하였습니다.

- Our main objective (in this study) was to measure nitrates in rivers.
- The main aim (of this research) was to investigate nitrates in rivers.
- We wanted to analyze the levels of nitrates in rivers.

Note A quick and easy way of restating objectives is with the verb wanted.

- We wanted to analyse levels of nitrates, and we also wanted to test methods of reducing nitrates.

You can use the word wanted several times to introduce a number of objectives.

연구 목적을 되짚어 볼 때는 세 번째 예문과 같이 wanted를 사용하는 것이 가장 간단하다. 목적이 여러 개일 경우에 wanted를 반복적으로 사용할 수 있다.

5 Restate research questions
의문 · 가설을 다시 한번 말한다

It will help the audience if your **conclusion slide refers back to the research questions** that were posed at the beginning of the presentation.

이 연구를 통해 어떤 의문(research questions)에 답을 찾으려고 했는지, 어떤 가설을 검증하려고 했는지 다시 한번 설명한다. 필요에 따라 의문 · 가설을 슬라이드에 넣는 것도 좋은 방법이다.

(슬라이드를 보여 주면서) 이 연구에서는 이러한 의문에 답을 찾으려고 했습니다.

- **This is just to remind you of our research questions. What are the sources of nitrates in rivers** and **how can they be reduced?**
  (In this example and the ones that follow, research questions can be shown on the slide if necessary)
- **This was our research question.**
- **These were our research questions.**
- **I'd just like to remind you of our research questions, which were as follows.**
- **This was our research hypothesis.**
- **This was our hypothesis.**
- **So, our research hypothesis was that** sunlight is a reliable method of degrading polymers.

Example of functions 1-5

This is a combined example of functions 1-5. It shows how to start the summary of your presentation with just a few sentences.

Script(1~5를 차례대로 연결한 원고의 예)

This is my last slide. We have been working on ways of improving water quality, and looked at water pollution in agricultural areas. We wanted to analyse the level of nitrates. Our research question was: How can nitrates be controlled effectively?

2 Introduce the findings, implications, and future work: Steps 6-11
연구 결과의 요점이나 청중에게 보내는 메시지를 말한다: 6~11단계

6 Introduce the findings
결과를 요약한다

Script(결과 요약의 예)

① Here are the results from the 15 institutions caring for the elderly that implemented the study program. ② We found that the average number of falls per patient decreased by more than 20 percent. ③ We also found that there was an improvement in patient mobility, balance, and general fitness. ④ Additionally, we found an increase in patients' wellbeing and general happiness.

Key sentences

6.1 Signal the start of the findings
결과의 요점을 정리하겠다는 의사 표현을 한다

The presenter begins by signaling the start of the findings.

이것이 이 연구의 주요 결과입니다.

- Here are the results from the 15 institutions caring for the elderly that implemented the study program.

결과를 요약하겠다는 의사 표현은 왼쪽과 같이 말한다.

Examples

- These are the findings / main results / main points from the program.
- These are our main findings.

6.2 Stating the findings 결과의 요점을 언급한다

~인 것으로 밝혀졌습니다.

- **We found that** the average number of falls per patient decreased by more than 20 percent.

Examples

- **Results showed that** there was a 20 percent reduction in falls.
- **So, what we saw was** a 20 percent reduction in falls.
- **So, we saw** a 20 percent reduction in falls.
- **There was** a 20 percent reduction in falls.

결과의 요점을 We found that ~ 등의 능동태 문장으로 표현한다.

6.3 Introducing more findings
결과의 다른 요점을 언급한다(1)

또, ~라는 것도 알았습니다.

- **We also found that** there was an improvement in patient mobility, balance, and general fitness.

Examples

- **The other thing (that) we found was that** patient mobility, balance, and general fitness improved.

여러 개의 결과를 소개하는 경우에는 also, additionally, the other thing (that) we found was that ~ 등의 표현을 활용한다.

6.4 Introducing additional findings
결과의 추가적인 요점도 언급한다(2)

또한, ~에 대해서도 알게 되었습니다.

- **Additionally, we found** an increase in patients' wellbeing and general happiness.

Examples

- **Additionally, we found that** there was an increase in patients' wellbeing and general happiness.
- **Another thing we found was** an increase in patients' wellbeing and general happiness.

Note Presenters frequently use the following sentences to introduce their findings. It was suggested that, It was concluded that, It was thought that. These expressions are too formal for oral presentations and are used in written academic English only. It is better to introduce the findings with an active sentence starting with we. For example, We found that, We also found that.

결과를 소개할 때 It was suggested that ~ 등의 수동태 표현을 사용하면 논문처럼 딱딱한 느낌을 준다. 구두발표에서는 We found that ~, We also found that ~ 등의 we로 시작하는 능동태 문장으로 말한다.

7 Explain the findings
결과로부터 얻을 수 있는 결론을 요약하여 언급한다

It is common for presenters to make **a general statement about their research findings**. This is a kind of overview that **puts the results in perspective** and gives the audience a more **global picture of the significance of the research/study**.

주요 결과를 소개한 후에 이로부터 어떤 일반적인 결론을 끌어낼 수 있는지 등을 고찰한다.

7.1 Introduce the start of the explanation
결론을 설명하겠다는 말머리를 꺼낸다

Here the presenter signals the start of a general statement about the meaning of the results.

결과를 요약하겠다는 의사 표현으로 왼쪽과 같이 말한다. 의문형을 활용하면 청중의 관심을 모을 수 있다.

이 결과들은 무엇을 의미할까요?

- **So, what do these results mean?**

Examples

- **What is the significance of these findings?**
- **What is the meaning of these results?**
- **I'll summarize the significance of these results.**

7.2 Main message 결론을 요약하여 설명한다

At this point, the presenter makes a comment on the findings presented so far in the form of a main message. Here are some useful expressions.

이 결과는 ~을 나타내고 있습니다.

- **Taken together, these results tell us that** action taken at grass-roots level by local staff makes a significant difference in terms of a reduction in the number of falls, and also an increase in general health and wellbeing.

Examples

- **Taken together, these findings suggest that** action taken at grass-roots level by staff has more significant effects on patient wellbeing than top-down directives.
- **Taken as a whole, this material shows** that action taken at grass-roots level by staff has more significant effects on patient wellbeing than top-down directives.
- **Overall, these data indicate that** action taken at grass-roots level by staff has more significant effects on patient wellbeing than top-down directives.
- **All in all, these findings indicate that** action taken at grass-roots level by staff on the ground has more significant effects on patient wellbeing than top-down directives.

'이러한 결과들을 요약하면'이라고 말할 때는 **taken together**, **taken as a whole**, **overall**, **all in all** 등의 표현을 사용한다. '이러한 결과들은 ~을 나타내고 있습니다'는 **these results tell us that ~** 또는 **these findings suggest that ~** 등으로 표현한다.

Note A good way of emphasizing the main message is with the expressions, **Taken together**, **Taken as a whole, overall, all in all**. Please note that the verb in these sentences is in the present tense: **tell**, **suggest**, **show**, **indicate**. However, when you introduce the results the verb will be in the past tense. For example, **We found / We observed**. The verbs are in the past tense.

결과를 표현할 때 사용하는 동사로 **tell**, **suggest**, **show**, **indicate** 등이 있다. 결과를 소개할 때는 과거형으로 말하지만, 결과로부터 얻을 수 있는 결론을 설명할 때는 현재형으로 표현해야 한다.

8 State the take-home message
청중에게 가장 전하고 싶은 핵심적인 메시지를 말한다

The take-home message is the main finding expressed as clearly as possible. It is the message that the presenter wants the audience to remember.

Take-home message는 청중이 집에 돌아갈 때 꼭 가져가기를 바라는 가장 중요한 메시지이며, 그 발표에서 가장 전하고 싶은 내용을 말한다.

오늘 발표의 핵심적인 메시지는 ~입니다.

- **This is the take-home message.** Local initiatives involving staff are more effective than top-down directives.

Examples

- **So, the take-home message is that** the numbers of falls can be significantly reduced by involving staff in the decision-making process.
- **Here is the take-home message.** Local initiatives involving staff are more effective than top-down directives.
- **Here is the take-away message.** The number of falls can be significantly reduced by involving staff on the ground in the decision-making process.

Note The expression **take-home message** means **take-away message**. Although the pattern is different, there is no difference in meaning. The expression **take-home message is more frequently used than take-away message.**

Take-home message는 **take-away message**라고도 하지만, 일반적으로 **take-home message**라는 용어를 더 흔히 사용한다.

9 Mention the implications
연구의 의의를 말한다

The word implications refers to the impact of the findings on the field. Here is an example.

마지막으로 이 연구의 결과가 해당 학문 분야에서 어떤 의의가 있는지, 실용적이나 임상적인 측면에서 어떻게 활용할 수 있는지 등을 설명한다.

Script(연구의 의의를 기술하는 예)

① What are the implications of these results? ② The main one is the obvious importance of local initiatives.

이 연구의 결과는 어떤 의의가 있을까요?

- What are the implications of these results?

Examples

- What are the cost / nursing implications?
- What are the implications of this study for healthcare of elderly people in institutions?

특히 중요한 점은 ~라는 것입니다.

- The main one is the obvious importance of local initiatives.

Examples

- Local initiatives at the grass root level are more effective, cost less and help to keep staff motivated.
- The main implication is that bottom-up initiatives involving front line staff are more effective in terms of cost and patient wellbeing than top-down directives.
- I think it is clear that initiatives at grass root level are more effective in terms of cost and patient wellbeing than top-down directives.

10 Finishing with the expressions: I hope that, That's what I wanted to tell you about + topic, That's what I wanted to say about + topic 요약을 끝낸다

In some cases, presenters use the following sentences to finish their presentations.

다음으로는 향후의 연구 과제에 대한 언급이나 사례 등이 남아 있는데, 발표의 본론 요약은 이것으로 끝낸다. 요약을 마친다는 표현은 왼쪽과 같이 말한다.

● I hope that this information has been of interest

오늘 발표에 관심이 있으셨기를 바랍니다.

- I hope that you have found this data interesting.
- I hope that this presentation will promote interest in this largely under-researched field.
- I hope that this presentation will encourage others to look at ways of creating a safe environment in care homes.

I hope that ~이라는 표현을 사용하여 '발표에 관심이 있으셨기를 바랍니다', '이 발표가 ~에 관심을 갖는 계기가 되었으면 좋겠습니다'와 같은 방식으로 마무리한다.

● That is what I wanted to tell you today about (topic)

오늘 말씀은 이것으로 마치겠습니다.

- That is what I wanted to tell you today. I hope you found this data interesting.
- That is what I wanted to tell you about creating a safe environment in care homes.

That is what I wanted to tell you today about ~ 또는 That is what I wanted to say about ~ 등의 표현으로 오늘의 발표 내용이 마무리되었음을 밝힌다.

● That is what I wanted to say about (topic)

이상이 오늘 말씀드린 내용입니다.

- That's what I wanted to say about (topic). I hope that you found this talk interesting.
- That is what I wanted to say about creating a safe environment in care homes.
- That is what I wanted to say about patient care. I think this aspect of care for the elderly deserves more attention.

- That is what I wanted to say about patient care. I think this aspect of care merits more attention.
- That is what I wanted to say about patient care. I think this aspect of care necessitates further research/study.
- That is what I wanted to say today. I hope you found this data interesting.
- Those were/are the points I wanted to make today.

11 Future work / Future directions
이후의 연구 과제를 말한다

Most presenters include a statement about future work. The following sentences signal that you will talk about future work.

간략히 발표 내용을 요약한 후에 이후의 연구 과제에 대해서도 간단하게 소개한다.

앞으로 진행할 연구 과제에 대해서도 간단히 말씀드리겠습니다.
저희는 앞으로 ~을 할 예정입니다.

- I'd (just) like to mention (our) future work. We plan to do further experiments with lasers.
- I'll (just) say a few words about future directions. We plan to do further experiments with lasers.
- As for future work, we plan to do further experiments using lasers.
- In terms of future work, we plan to do further experiments using lasers.
- Concerning future work, we plan to do further experiments using lasers.

Note In the above examples, the following 3 expressions are used to introduce future work: As for future work, In terms of future work, Concerning future work,

향후의 연구 과제를 소개할 때는 As for future work, In terms of future work, Concerning future work 등의 표현을 활용한다.

Here I show how to give examples of future work using the following verbs: plan, want, is.

Plan

다음에는 ~을 시행할 예정입니다.

- We plan to do further experiments using lasers.
- We plan to do another study with more subjects focusing on a wider range of OTC whitening products.
- We are planning to investigate the use of laser technology.
- We are planning to do another study on the incidence of relapse in people using OTC whitening products.
- (As for future work), we are planning to do more experiments on how to refine the system with a laser.
- (Concerning future work), we are planning to do more experiments on how to refine the system with a laser.
- (In terms of future work), we plan to conduct further research on OTC whitening products.

Plan(동사)을 사용하여 We plan to do ~ 또는 We are planning to do ~ 등의 표현으로 향후의 연구 계획에 대해 언급한다.

> **Note** A common pattern is We plan to do more work / more experiments / another study on topic.

Want

앞으로는 ~에 대해 조사하려고 합니다.

- We want to take further samples at lower temperatures.
- We want to look at ways of reducing interference.
- We want to look at ways of overcoming the above problems associated with institutionalized adults.

Want라는 용어를 사용할 때는 We want to ~의 표현으로 앞으로 진행하려는 연구의 내용을 소개한다.

● Is (to)

다음 과제는 ~입니다.

- **The next step is to** refine the system with laser technology.
- **The next stage (in this research) is to** refine the system with laser technology.
- **Our next goal is to** achieve higher yields in terms of production.
- **What we want to do next is to** develop a more robust system that can be used in colder environments.

Is라는 용어를 사용할 때는 **is to** (+ 동사)의 표현으로 '다음 과제는 ~하는 것입니다'와 같이 말한다.

Note The expression **is to + verb** is usually preceded by the following expressions:

- **The next step**
- **The next stage**
- **Our next goal**
- **The next part of this research**
- **What we want to do next**
- **What we plan to do next**

+ is to + develop an improved system.

Please note the **usage of singular and plural** in the following expressions.

1. Usually singular: Future work, future research

The words **work** and **research** are not used in the plural.

2. Usually plural: Future plans, future projects, future experiments, future directions, future perspectives

The words **plans**, **projects**, **experiments**, **directions** and **perspectives** are generally plural when talking about future work.

'향후 과제' 또는 '다음의 연구 계획'이라고 말할 때는 **work**, **research**는 단수형으로, **plans**, **projects**, **experiments**, **directions**, **perspectives**는 복수형으로 표현한다.

3 Finishing the presentation: Steps 12-16
발표를 마친다: 12~16단계

12 Funding
연구비 지원에 관하여 언급한다

Recently, it is common for presenters to include information on funding.

최근에는, 발표가 끝날 때 연구비 지원에 관련된 언급을 하는 것이 일반적인 경향이다.

이 연구는 ○○기금의 연구 지원을 받아 시행하였습니다.

- This research/study/work was supported by a grant from the Ministry of Construction.
- I'd just like to mention that this research was supported by a grant from the Sato Foundation.
- For this research, we obtained funding from the Ministry of Education.
- For this research, we got funding from the Ministry of Education.

연구비 지원에 관해 언급할 때는 be supported by a grant from ~ 또는 we obtained/got funding from ~으로 말한다. Obtained라는 용어가 got보다는 격식 있는 정중한 표현이다.

Note The word obtained is more formal than got. Got is widely used as it is informal and easy to say.

(슬라이드에 작성한 연구비 지원 목록을 가리키면서)

이 연구는 이러한 연구비 지원을 받아 수행하였습니다.

- You can see our funding sources here. (Show a list of funding sources. It is not necessary to read them).
- Here are the sources of funding for this work. (Show a list of funding sources. It is not necessary to read them).

여러 연구비를 지원받았으면 슬라이드에 연구비 지원 목록 제시한 후에 왼쪽처럼 언급할 수 있다. 이렇게 하면 목록의 세부 사항을 일일이 열거하지 않아도 된다.

Note Funding is always singular. You cannot say *fundings*.

Funding은 항상 단수형으로 써야 하므로 *fundings*라고 하지 않도록 주의한다.

13 Acknowledgments
감사의 마음을 전한다

Here are some examples of how to introduce acknowledgments.

이 연구에 참여해 주신 여러분께 깊이 감사드립니다.

- **I wish to thank the following people.** (+ a list of names and a photo)

이어서 연구 협력자 또는 공동 연구자에게 감사를 표한다. 이때 동사는 thank 또는 acknowledge를 활용한다.

감사의 말을 할 때 슬라이드에 연구 협력자의 명단과 사진을 함께 보여 주는 것이 좋다.

Thank

- **I want to thank my coworkers at** the Institute of Health Science.
- **I'd like to thank my colleagues at** the Institute of Health Science.
- **I'd like to say a big thank you to** my coworkers at AIST.

Acknowledge

- **I'd like to acknowledge the following people.** (Show a list of people's names)

14 Signal the end of the presentation
마무리 인사를 한다

It is important to signal the end of the presentation clearly. The shortest way of doing this is to say, **Thank you**. This is short for **Thank you for your attention**. Another option is, **That's all I have to say**. Some presenters shorten this to ***That's all***, but this is too abrupt and rather informal.

Here are some examples.

청중에게 마무리 인사로 감사를 표한다. Thank you for your attention 또는 간단히 Thank you라고 한다.

Thank you 앞에 "오늘 발표는 여기까지입니다(That's all I have to say)."라고 말할 수도 있다.

오늘 발표는 여기까지입니다. 들어 주셔서 감사합니다.

- Thank you.
- Thank you very much.
- Thank you for your attention.
- Thank you very much for your attention.
- That's all I have to say. Thank you for your attention.
- That covers what I wanted to say today. Thank you for your attention.
- That covers what I wanted to say about (topic). Thank you for your attention.
- That concludes my presentation. Thank you for your attention.

Common errors — 흔히 하는 실수

✕ *Thanks.*
○ Thank you.
○ Thank you very much.

The word thanks is too informal and not suitable for an oral presentation at a conference.

*Thanks*라는 용어는 격식이 너무 없는 표현이므로 학회 발표에서는 피한다.

✕ *That's it.*
○ That is all I have to say.
○ That is all I have to say. Thank you for your attention.

The expression *That's it* is too informal for a conference presentation. If it is combined with another expression, it can be used, but it is still rather informal. For example, That's it. Thank you very much for your attention. Generally, I advise presenters to avoid the expression *That's it*.

*That's it*도 격식이 없는 표현이므로 학회 발표에서는 피한다. 다른 표현과 조합하여 That's it. Thank you very much for your attention 등으로 말할 수도 있지만 아무래도 격식 없는 느낌을 줄 수 있으므로 이런 표현은 사용하지 않는 편이 좋다.

✕ *That's all.*
✕ *That's all for my presentation.*
◯ Thank you.
◯ Thank you for your attention.
◯ That's all I have to say. Thank you for your time.
◯ That's all I have to say. Thank you for your attention.
◯ That concludes my presentation. Thank you.

That's all은 반드시 I have to say와 연결하여 That's all I have to say의 형태로 표현해야 한다. *That's all for my presentation*은 잘못된 표현이다.

I am surprised that so many presenters use these expressions. ***That's all.*** / ***That's all for my presentation***. Both are incorrect. If you use **That's all**, you must use the expression **I have to say**. For example, **That's all I have to say. Thank you for your attention**. Please avoid ***That's all for my presentation***. It is incorrect and makes a bad impression.

✕ Thank you for ***your*** listening.
◯ Thank you for listening.

'들어 주셔서 감사합니다'를 *Thank you for your listening*이라고 한다면 잘못된 표현이다. Your를 빼고 Thank you for listening이라고 하거나 Thank you for your attention이라고 해야 한다. Attention은 단수형으로 사용해야 하므로 주의한다.

In the above error, the problem is the expression ***your listening***. It is possible to say, **Thank you for your attention**. But, ***Thank you for your listening*** is not correct.

✕ Thank you for your ***attentions***.
◯ Thank you for your **attention**.

The word attention is always singular and never plural.

15 Contact details
발표자의 연락처를 알려준다

In some cases, presenters mention their contact details and show their email addres on the screen.

(슬라이드에 메일 주소를 표시하고) **이것이 제 연락처입니다.**
관심 있으신 분께서는 편하게 연락해 주시기 바랍니다.

- Here are my contact details. Please feel free to get in contact.
- Here are my contact details. If you are interested in this study or would like to have any more information, please get in contact.

발표자의 연락처를 소개할 때는 슬라이드에 이메일 주소를 표시하고, 왼쪽과 같이 말한다.

16 Invite questions
질문을 받는다

Most sessions have a chairperson who will handle the question and answer session. In these cases, it is unnecessary to invite questions. In cases where there is no chairperson, you can invite questions in the following way.

질문이 있습니까?

- I'd be happy to take any questions you might have.
- I'd be happy to answer any questions.
- I'll take questions now.
- Are there any questions or comments?
- Does anyone have any questions or comments?

청중에게 질문을 요청하는 것은 보통 좌장이 하는 일이지만, 좌장이 없을 때는 발표자가 다음과 같은 표현으로 스스로 질문을 받는다.

질문을 요청할 때 *Any question?*이라고 하면 안 되고, 복수형으로 Any questions?라고 해야 한다. 하지만 이 표현도 조금 격식이 떨어지므로 Are there any questions?라고 정중하게 표현하는 것이 좋다.

질문뿐 아니라 비평까지 덧붙여 questions or comments라고 요청할 수도 있다.

Note A lot of presenters and people who act as a chairperson use the following pattern. *Any question?* This is incorrect because the word question should be plural. Any questions? But this not a full sentence and sounds very casual. The full sentence is as follows: Are there any questions? Sometimes this is extended to, Are there any questions or comments? / Does anyone have any questions or comments?

Part 6

How to create a clear summary slide and an audience-friendly script

알기 쉬운 요약 슬라이드를 만드는 방법과 설명하는 방식

In this part, I show how to change an existing summary slide with several serious problems to an easy to understand slide with a script that supports the main points in the slide. You will see that the summary is changed from something that is too wordy and difficult to understand to something that is more accessible.

In this section, I cover 2 summary slides, each of which consists of 5 parts.

1. The slide before revision
2. How to make your slide more accessible by using less formal English
3. The revised slide
4. The script for introducing the information on the summary slide
5. Summary script: Functions and more examples

발표 마지막에는 '요약 슬라이드'를 제시하고 발표 내용의 요점을 정리한다. 이때 단순히 문장을 나열하는 슬라이드는 청중을 배려한 요약이라고 할 수 없다. 이 장에서는 두 가지 예를 통해 간결하고 보기 쉬운 요약 슬라이드를 만드는 방법을 제시한다. 또한, 요약 슬라이드를 설명할 때 사용할 원고의 작성 요령에 대해서도 함께 알아본다.

1 Summary slide example 1
요약 슬라이드의 수정 예 (1)

First, let's look at the summary slide in its original form. Please spend a minute or two reading through the material on the slide. Try to identify the main points that the presenter wants to make.

1.1 The slide before revision
수정하기 전의 요약 슬라이드

Summary

The authors found snacking significantly increases the child's risk of developing dental caries, in some cases in excess of 20 percent. The crucial factors in elevated risk of caries were established as frequency, that is to say, the number of times foods with high levels of sugar were consumed, and consistency of items consumed, that is thickness and smoothness. Moreover, risk of cavities depended to a greater degree on consistency than amount consumed. The role of sealants in preventing caries in early childhood will be the subject of a future study.

This summary slide has the following issues.

- There are too many words.
- There is too much information.
- There is no space between sentences.
- The main points are not clear.
- The English is too formal for an oral presentation.
- The audience will not have time to read or understand the information.

1.2 How to make your summary slide more accessible by using less formal English
격식을 차리지 않는 평범한 영어를 사용하여 읽기 쉬운 슬라이드로 수정하는 방법

One of the problems with this slide is that the **English is too formal**. Here I show how to **reduce the formality of the English and create a slide that is simple and easy to follow**. In the examples below, the original sentence is shown. Next, **formal expressions are shown on the left** and **less formal expressions on the right**. After that, **the revised sentence is shown in full**.

이전 페이지의 요약 슬라이드는 문장이 길고 정보가 많아서 청중들이 읽기 어렵고, 요점을 파악할 수도 없을 뿐 아니라, 사용하는 영어도 논문에서 쓰는 딱딱한 표현이어서 학회 발표에는 적합하지 않다.

The authors found snacking significantly increases the child's risk of developing dental caries, in some cases in excess of 20 percent.

Formal expressions		Less formal expressions
The authors found	→	We found that
significantly increases	→	increases a lot
the child's risk of developing dental caries	→	the child's risk of getting tooth decay
in excess of 20 percent.	→	by more than 20 percent

We found that snacking increases the child's risk of getting tooth decay a lot, in some cases by more than 20 percent.

The crucial factors in elevated risk of caries were established as frequency, that is to say, the number of times foods with high levels of sugar were consumed, and consistency of items consumed, that is thickness and smoothness.

Formal expressions		Less formal expressions
▮ The crucial factors	→	▮ The important issues/points
▮ in elevated risk of caries	→	▮ in increased risk of decay
▮ were established as frequency	→	▮ were frequency ▮ were found to be frequency

Note The expression **established as** has been deleted. The revised phrases are as follows: **were frequency** / **were found to be frequency**

▮ that is to say	→	▮ in other words
▮ were consumed	→	▮ were eaten
▮ and consistency of items consumed	→	▮ and the texture of snacks eaten
▮ that is	→	▮ that means ▮ in other words

The important issues in increased risk of decay were frequency, in other words, the number of times snacks with high levels of sugar were eaten and the texture of the snack eaten, that means thickness and consistency.

Moreover, risk of cavities depended to a greater degree on consistency than amount consumed.

Formal expressions		Less formal expressions
Moreover	→	Also In addition
cavities	→	decay
to a greater degree on	→	more on
consumed	→	eaten

Also risk of decay depended more on consistency / texture than the amount eaten.

The role of sealants in preventing caries in early childhood will be the subject of a future study.

Formal expressions		Less formal expressions
will be the subject of a future study	→	As for future work, we plan to do a study on

As for future work, we plan to do a study on sealants as a way of preventing tooth decay in children.

1.3 The revised slide
수정한 후의 요약 슬라이드

Below you will see the revised slide, which now consists of notes on all the main points.

Summary

- Snacking **increases the risk of caries** in children
- Sometimes **in excess of 20 percent**
- Factors affecting risk: **1. frequency 2. consistency**
- **Risk depends more on consistency than amount eaten**
- **Future work: Using sealants as a way of preventing tooth decay** in children

1.4 Script for explaining the information on the summary slide
요약 슬라이드를 설명할 때 사용하는 원고

This is the script for the summary slide. It is shown as a single paragraph.

Script(요약 슬라이드 설명용 원고의 예)

① I would like to finish with a brief summary. ② We looked at the effect of snacking on risk of children getting tooth decay. ③ We found that snacking increases the child's risk of getting tooth decay. In some cases, this can be more than 20 percent. ④ We also found that there are two main factors that seem to affect risk. One is frequency. This means, the number of times the child snacks. ⑤ The other is consistency of the snack. Consistency, as I have already mentioned, is related to how much of the snack gets stuck between the teeth and attached to the surface of the teeth. ⑥ Finally, I'd like to stress that our results show that consistency is a greater risk than the amount of snacks eaten. ⑦ As for future work, we plan to do a study on sealants as a way of preventing tooth decay in children. ⑩ That's all I have to say. Thank you for your attention.

1.5 Summary script: functions and more examples
요약 슬라이드를 설명할 때 사용하는 원고의 예문

Here the main functions used to explain the summary slide are listed with further examples.

앞쪽의 요약 슬라이드 설명용 원고에서 각 문장과 비슷한 의미이지만 이를 다르게 표현하는 방법을 예문으로 소개한다. 요약을 설명할 때 사용하는 표현에 대해서는 Part 5의 자세한 해설과 예문을 참고한다.

1. Signal the start of the summary 요약을 시작하겠다는 말머리를 꺼낸다

이제 요약하겠다는 의사 표현은 왼쪽과 같이 말한다.

마지막으로, 앞선 발표 내용을 요약하고 오늘의 발표를 마무리하겠습니다.

- I would like to finish with a brief summary.

Examples

- This is my last slide.
- This is a summary.

2. Remind the audience of the study aims
연구의 목적을 돌이켜본다

연구의 목적을 재차 언급함으로써 청중이 발표의 전체적인 흐름을 쉽게 상기할 수 있다.

이 연구의 목적은 ~하는 것이었습니다.

- We looked at the effect of snacking on risk of children getting tooth clecay.

Examples

- We studied the effect of snacking on risk of children getting tooth clecay.
- We focused on the effect of snacking on risk of children getting tooth clecay.
- We investigated the effect of snacking on risk of children getting tooth clecay.

3. Introduce the main findings 주요 결과를 언급한다

이어서, 이 연구로 밝혀진 주요 결과를 제시한다.

~인 것으로 밝혀졌습니다.

- We found that snacking increases the child's risk of getting tooth decay. In some cases, this can be more than 20 percent.

Examples

- **This data shows that** snacking increases the child's risk of getting tooth decay. In some cases, this can be more than 20 percent.
- **So, the data shown here tells us that** snacking increases the risk of tooth decay in children. In some cases, this can be more than 20 percent.
- **So, the information shown here means that** snacking increases the risk of tooth decay in children. In some cases, this can be more than 20 percent.
- **So, the data shown here indicates that** snacking increases the risk of caries in children. In some cases, this can be more than 20 percent.
- **From this study, we concluded that** snacking increases the risk of caries in children. In some cases, this can be more than 20 percent.

4. Introduce more detailed findings (1)

결과를 더 자세히 소개한다 (1)

또 ~이라는 것도 밝혀졌습니다.

- **We also found that** there are two main factors that seem to affect risk.

또 다른 내용에 대해서 언급할 경우는 We also found ~ 또는 In addition 등의 표현을 활용한다.

Examples

- **In addition, we found that** there are two main factors that seem to affect risk.
- **Additionally, we found that** there are two main factors that seem to affect risk.
- **Another thing that we found was that** there are two main factors that seem to affect risk.

이것은 바꾸어 말하면, ~라는 것입니다.

- One is frequency. **This means,** the number of times the child snacks.

Examples

- **In other words,** the number of times the child snacks.
- **Frequency refers to** the number of times the child snacks.

전문 용어 등을 다른 말로 바꾸어 설명할 때는 왼쪽과 같이 말한다.

5. Introduce more detailed findings (2)

결과를 더 자세히 소개한다 (2)

1. Adding another point

다른 요인으로 ~이 있습니다.

- **The other (factor) is** consistency of the snack.

Examples

- **The other issue is** consistency of the snack.
- **The other key factor is** consistency of the snack.

2. Reminding the audience of information already presented

앞서 말씀드린 대로, ~.

- Consistency, **as I have already mentioned,** is related to how much of the snack gets stuck between the teeth and attached to the surface of the teeth.

Examples

- **As I said,** consistency of the snack is related to how much of the snack gets stuck between the teeth and attached to the surface of the teeth.
- **As I told you** consistency of the snack is related to how much of the snack gets stuck between the teeth and attached to the surface of the teeth.
- **As I pointed out,** consistency of the snack is related to how much of the snack gets stuck between the teeth and attached to the surface of the teeth.

이미 설명한 내용을 다시 언급할 때는 **As I have already mentioned,** 또는 **As I said,**에 이어서 말한다.

6. Introduce the main message 청중에게 가장 전하고 싶은 핵심 내용을 말한다

특히 중요한 내용은 ~입니다.

- Finally, I'd like to stress that our results show that consistency is a greater risk than the amount of snacks eaten.

이는 청중에게 가장 강조해서 전하고 싶은 부분으로, 이를 take-home message라고도 한다.

Examples

- Our main finding was that consistency is a greater risk than the amount of snacks eaten.
- The most important finding was that consistency is a greater risk than the amount of snacks eaten.
- The key finding was that consistency is a greater risk than the amount of snacks eaten.
- The take-home message is that consistency is a greater risk than the amount of snacks eaten.

7. Introduce future work 이후의 연구 과제를 말한다

앞으로는 ~에 관한 연구를 진행할 예정입니다.

- As for future work, we plan to do a study on sealants as a way of preventing tooth decay in children.

요약의 맨 마지막은 이번 연구 결과를 바탕으로 앞으로 어떤 연구를 진행할 것인지 소개한다.

Examples

- I'd just like to mention (our) future research plans. We plan to carry out further tests on the effects of sealing teeth in young children.
- I'd just like to mention that we are now conducting a further study on prevention of tooth decay in children using sealants.
- The aim of our future work is to conduct further tests on the effects of sealing teeth in young children.
- As for future work, we plan to do a study on sealants as a way of preventing tooth decay in children.
- The next step in this research is to carry out further tests on the effects of sealing teeth in young children.

8. Acknowledgments 감사의 말

> **Note** Functions 8~10 are not included in the summary slide, but I have listed them here because they are useful examples.

8~10은 요약 슬라이드에 포함되지는 않지만, 요약과 마찬가지로 발표의 마지막 부분에 언급하는 내용이다.

이 연구에 협력해 주신 여러분께 깊이 감사드립니다.

- I want to thank the people who have been involved in this work. (show a list of people's names and a photo)

공동 연구자 또는 연구에 참여한 사람들에게 감사의 마음을 전한다. 이때 공동 연구자의 명단과 사진을 슬라이드에 함께 넣으면 좋다.

Examples

- I would like to thank my coworkers who have contributed to this work.
- I'd like to acknowledge my coworkers who have contributed to this work.

9. Mention funding 연구비 지원에 대한 언급

이 연구는 ○○기금의 연구비 지원을 받아 진행하였습니다.

- This research was funded by the Ministry of Health, Welfare and Labor.

연구비 지원을 받아 수행한 연구는 지원 기관의 명칭 등을 언급한다.

Examples

- For this project we are getting funding from the Dutch Program for Tissue Engineering.
- We gratefully acknowledge the financial support of Lion Corporation.

10. Thank the audience 청중에게 인사

발표를 들어 주셔서 감사합니다.

- That's all I have to say. Thank you for your attention.

마지막으로 청중에게 감사 인사를 하고 발표를 모두 마무리한다.

Examples

- That concludes my presentation. Thank you.
- That covers everything I wanted to say. Thank you for your attention.

2 Summary slide example 2
요약 슬라이드의 수정 예 (2)

Let's start by looking at the slide in its original form. Please read through the information on the slide and identify the main points.

2.1 The summary slide before revision
수정하기 전의 요약 슬라이드

Summary

Our objective was to improve the physical and mental health of at risk people in areas with high levels of social issues.

Low-cost interventions for cardio-vascular disease and diabetes were investigated. Exercise, diet, and general health were focused on. Online and face-to-face materials were developed, including questionnaires, apps, automated reminders and community spaces, all of which could be accessed and submitted online.

It was found that after 6 months the following improved: mood, energy levels, mental function, blood pressure and BMI.

It was concluded that low-cost interventions focusing on at risk patients are effective in reducing the risk of serious diseases such as heart disease and diabetes. It was also suggested that low-cost interventions could be used effectively in combination with standard treatments. Ways of increasing patient access to low-cost interventions are currently being studied.

2.2 How to make the summary slide more accessible by using less formal English
격식을 차리지 않는 평범한 영어를 사용하여 읽기 쉬운 슬라이드로 고치는 방법

Our objective was to improve the physical and mental health of at risk people in areas with high levels of social issues.

Formal expressions	Informal expressions
Our objective was to improve	We wanted to improve Our aim was to improve

We wanted to improve the physical and mental health of at risk people in areas with high levels of social issues.

Low-cost interventions for cardio-vascular disease and diabetes were investigated.

Formal expressions	Informal expressions
were investigated	We looked at low-cost interventions We focused on low-cost interventions We investigated low-cost interventions We studied low-cost interventions

We looked at low-cost interventions for cardio-vascular disease and diabetes.

Exercise, diet, and general health were focused on.

Formal expressions	Informal expressions
were focused on	We looked at We focused on

We also looked at exercise, diet, and general health.

Online and face-to-face materials were developed, including questionnaires, apps, automated reminders and community spaces, all of which could be accessed and submitted online.

Formal expressions	Informal expressions
were developed	We made We created

We made online and face-to-face materials, including questionnaires, apps, automated reminders and community spaces, all of which could be accessed and submitted online.

It was found that after 6 months the following improved: mood, energy levels, mental function, blood pressure and BMI.

Formal expressions	Informal expressions
It was found that	We found that We concluded that

We found that after 6 months the following improved: mood, energy levels, mental function, blood pressure and BMI.

It was concluded that low-cost interventions focusing on at risk patients are effective in reducing the risk of serious diseases such as heart disease and diabetes.

Formal expressions		Informal expressions
▪ It was concluded	→	▪ We found that ▪ We concluded that

We found that low-cost interventions focusing on at risk patients are effective in reducing the risk of serious diseases such as heart disease and diabetes.

It was also suggested that low-cost interventions could be used effectively in combination with standard treatments.

Formal expressions		Informal expressions
▪ It was also suggested	→	▪ We also found ▪ Additionally, we found

Additionally, we found that low-cost interventions could be used effectively in combination with standard treatments.

Ways of increasing patient access to low-cost interventions are currently being studied.

Formal expressions		Informal expressions
▪ are currently being studied	→	▪ We are now working on ways of

We are now working on ways of increasing patient access to low-cost interventions.

2.3 The revised slide
수정한 후의 요약 슬라이드

Summary

Aims Improve the physical and mental health of at risk people in areas with high levels of social issues.

Approach Investigate the benefits of low-cost online approaches to interventions for diseases such as heart disease and diabetes, focusing on exercise, diet and general health.

Online interventions Questionnaires, apps, automated reminders, communal online support spaces.

Health benefits After 6 months, the following improved: mood, energy levels, mental functions, blood pressure and BMI.

Take-home message Low-cost online interventions are effective in reducing the risk of serious diseases such as heart disease and diabetes, and can be used effectively in combination with standard treatments.

Future directions How to increase patient access to low-cost interventions.

2.4 Script for introducing the summary slide
요약 슬라이드를 설명할 때 사용하는 원고

Here is the script for introducing the information on the above slide.

Script(요약 슬라이드 설명용 원고의 예)

① This is a summary. ② We wanted to improve the physical and mental health of at risk people in areas with high levels of social issues. ③ We looked at the benefits of low-cost online approaches and face-to-face interventions for CVD and diabetes, focusing on exercise, diet, and general health.

④ We used online interviews as well as questionnaires, apps, automated reminders and community spaces. ⑤ Here are the main results. We found that after 6 months, the following improved: mood, energy levels, blood pressure and BMI. ⑥ This is the main message. We found that low-cost interventions focusing on at risk individuals were effective in reducing the risk of heart disease, diabetes and other serious diseases. ⑦ Additionally, we found that low-cost interventions could be used effectively in combination with standard treatments. ⑧ I'd like to mention future directions. We are now working on ways of increasing patient access to low-cost interventions.

2.5 Summary script: functions and examples
요약 슬라이드를 설명할 때 사용하는 원고의 예문

1. Signal the start of the summary 요약을 시작하겠다는 말머리를 꺼낸다

오늘 발표의 요약입니다.

- This is a summary.

Examples

- This is my last slide.
- I'd like to go over the main points.
- These are the main points I covered today.
- I'm going to summarize my presentation.

요약의 각 단계에서 활용하는 표현에 대해서는 요약 슬라이드의 수정 예 (1)(214~219쪽)과 Part 5를 참고한다.

'이제 요약하겠다'는 의사 표현은 왼쪽과 같이 말한다.

2. Restate the objectives 연구의 목적을 돌이켜본다

~을 목적으로 이 연구를 시행했습니다.

- **We wanted to** improve the physical and mental health of at risk people in areas with high levels of social issues.

처음에, 연구의 목적을 상기한다.

Examples

- **The main aim was to** find ways to improve the physical and mental health of at risk people in areas with high levels of social issues.
- **We looked at** ways of improving the physical and mental health of at risk people in areas with high levels of social issues.

3. Introduce the topic 연구 주제를 언급한다

~에 대해서, 특히 ~을 중심으로 조사했습니다.

- **We looked at** the benefits of low-cost online approaches and face-to-face interventions for CVD and diabetes, **focusing on** exercise, diet, and general health.

발표 주제를 다시 한번 언급한다.

Examples

- **We analyzed** the benefits of low-cost online approaches and face-to-face interventions for CVD and diabetes, **focusing on** exercise, diet, and general health.
- **We investigated** the benefits of low-cost online approaches and face-to-face interventions for CVD and diabetes, **focusing on** exercise, diet, and general health.
- **We assessed** the benefits of low-cost online approaches and face-to-face interventions for CVD and diabetes, **focusing on** exercise, diet, and general health.
- **We considered** the benefits of low-cost online approaches and face-to-face interventions for CVD and diabetes, **focusing on** exercise, diet, and general health.

4. Introduce the methods 연구 방법을 언급한다

~이라는 기법을 이용했습니다.

- We used online interviews as well as questionnaires, apps, automated reminders and community spaces.

Examples

- We employed online interviews as well as questionnaires, apps, automated reminders and community spaces.
- We made use of online interviews as well as questionnaires, apps, automated reminders and community spaces.

연구 방법을 간단히 되짚어 본다.

5. Introduce the results 연구 결과를 언급한다

이것이 주된 결과입니다.

- Here are the main results. (We found that) after 6 months, the following improved: mood, energy levels, blood pressure and BMI.

Examples

- These are the main results. After 6 months, the following improved: mood, energy levels, blood pressure and BMI.
- This is what we found. We found that after 6 months, the following improved: mood, energy levels, blood pressure and BMI.
- These are the main findings. (We found that) after 6 months, the following improved: mood, energy levels, blood pressure and BMI.
- I'll just run through the main results. (We found that) after 6 months, the following improved: mood, energy levels, blood pressure and BMI.
- I'll just go over the main results. (We found that) after 6 months, the following improved: mood, energy levels, blood pressure and BMI.

연구 결과에서 주요 내용을 간결하게 언급한다.

6. Introduce the main message 청중에게 강조하는 핵심적인 메시지를 말한나

특히 중요한 것은 ~입니다.

- This is the main message. (We found that) low-cost interventions focusing on at risk individuals were effective in reducing the risk of heart disease, diabetes and other serious diseases.

연구 결과를 바탕으로 청중에게 특히 강조하여 전하고 싶은 것(take-home message)을 말한다.

Examples

- This is the take-home message. (We found that) low-cost interventions focusing on at risk individuals were effective in reducing the risk of heart disease, diabetes and other serious diseases.
- Taken together, these results show that low-cost interventions focusing on at risk individuals are effective in reducing the risk of heart disease, diabetes and other serious diseases.
- We concluded that low-cost interventions focusing on at risk individuals are effective in reducing the risk of heart disease, diabetes and other serious diseases.

7. Add additional results 추가 결과를 언급한다

또한, ~라는 것도 알았습니다.

- Additionally, we found that low-cost interventions could be used effectively in combination with standard treatments.

다른 중요한 결과도 언급한다

Examples

- We also think that such interventions can be used effectively in combination with standard treatments.
- We also feel that such interventions can be used effectively in combination with standard treatments.
- These results also suggest / show that such interventions can be used effectively in combination with standard treatments.

8. Refer to future work 이후의 연구에 관해 말한다

앞으로 수행할 연구에 대해서도 말씀드리겠습니다. 현재 저희는 ~에 관한 연구를 진행하고 있습니다.

- I'd like to mention future directions. We are now working on ways of increasing patient access to low-cost interventions.

Examples

- I'd just like to mention future directions. We plan to carry out a study on ways of increasing patient access to low-cost interventions.
- I'll just say a few words about future directions. We plan to carry out a study on ways of increasing patient access to low-cost interventions.
- As for future directions, we plan to carry out a further study on ways of increasing patient access to low-cost interventions.
- In terms of future work, we plan to carry out a further study on ways of increasing patient access to low-cost interventions.
- The next step in this research is to carry out a study on ways of increasing patient access to low-cost interventions.

마지막으로, 이후의 연구 과제나 현재 진행 중인 연구의 개요에 대해서도 언급한다.

9. Finish the presentation 발표를 마친다

이상으로 오늘 발표를 마칩니다. 들어주셔서 감사합니다.

- That's all I have to say. Thank you for your attention.

Examples

- Thank you.
- Thank you for your time.
- Thank you very much for your attention.

발표를 매듭지을 때는 왼쪽과 같이 말한다.